BFI   TV Classics

BFI T✓ Classics is a series of books celebrating key individual television progrmmes and series. Television scholars, critics and novelists provide critical readings underpinned with careful research, alongside a personal respose to the programme and a case for its 'classic' status.

Acknowledgments

I owe a debt of thanks to many past and present BFI colleagues for support, advice and encouragement during the writing of this book, particularly Richard Paterson, Bryony Dixon, Danny Birchall, Megan Skinner, Jacinta Philips, Kathleen Dickson, Tise Vahimagi and Julian Grainger. I am especially grateful to Rebecca Barden and Sophia Contento at BFI Publishing for their dedication and patience. My profound thanks go to Jimmy McGovern and Gub Neal, who gave generously of their time and offered many fascinating and revealing insights. Finally, I am forever indebted to Eleni Liarou, who helped me see the wood for the trees and the trees for the wood. This book is for her, and for my father, whose own shining example fostered my fascination with television.

Introduction

At the end of Warner Bros.' *Angels with Dirty Faces* (1938), Jimmy
Cagney's Rocky Sullivan, a juvenile delinquent-turned-gangster who has
fatefully returned to the ghetto neighbourhood of his youth, has reached
the end of his wayward journey and now faces the electric chair.
Rocky is visited on death row by his childhood cohort, Jerry
(Pat O'Brien), now a Catholic priest, who is desperate to deter the
impressionable young boys under his tutelage from taking the Rocky
road, and begs his former friend to make a show of cowardice in his last
moments to break the spell he has over them. Rocky, out of pride,
refuses, and walks stoutly to the place of his appointed death. But at the
last he undergoes an apparent transformation, and has to be dragged
screaming to the chair; as the newspaper headline puts it, he 'dies
yellow'. Hearing this, the boys' illusions are shattered.

  The scene is one of classical Hollywood's most enigmatic.
The unanswered question is whether Rocky's last cries betray
unexpected but genuine fear, or whether, as Father Jerry believes, they
are an act for the benefit of the boys: cowardice or altruism.
Doctor Edward Fitzgerald, brought to life by Robbie Coltrane and
known to all as Fitz, the psychologist hero of *Cracker* (ITV,
1993–2006), favours the second view: Father Jerry's heartfelt plea and
memories of his own hopeless childhood awaken in Rocky a desire to do
one good deed before his death. But Fitz's wife, Judith (Barbara Flynn),
offers a third interpretation: as a Catholic, Rocky has only one faint
hope of saving his soul: he must *do as his priest has instructed him*.

His ultimate act, then, is born not of altruism, but of selfishness – it is not for the boys' future, but his own.

This discussion occupies barely a minute of *Cracker*'s third story, 'One Day a Lemming Will Fly', and ostensibly shows Fitz and Judith sharing a rare moment of calm companionship in the near-constant tempest of their marriage. But the debate crystallises most of *Cracker*'s touchstone themes: justice and injustice, Catholicism, moral choices and the impossibility of a 'pure motive', the after-effects of death. *Cracker*, what's more, has something of the tenor of the 1930s Warner Bros. pictures, with their stories 'torn from the headlines', taking the temperature of early 90s Britain much as films like *Angels with Dirty Faces* or *I Am a Fugitive from a Chain Gang* (1932) did for America in the 30s. Another Warner Bros. title, *They Made Me a Criminal* (1939), could even describe one of *Cracker*'s stories. Fitz, perhaps, likes to imagine himself as one of the studio's from-the-streets antiheroes embodied by Cagney or Humphrey Bogart – a portrait of Bogart hangs in his study, while he is fond of mimicking Cagney's distinctive voice and dialogue. It was Bogart, of course, who so completely incarnated those 'hardboiled' detectives, culled from the pages of Chandler and Hammett, who would do so much for Warner Bros.' balance sheets in the 1940s, and who form one part of Fitz's complex identity.

When *Cracker* had its first outing in September 1993, television audiences were not exactly poorly served for crime stories. Police in or out of uniform slugged it out with petty criminals most weeknights in *The Bill* (ITV, 1984–), and the ITV schedules in particular were full to bursting with detectives of one kind or another, whether active or resting: *Inspector Morse* (ITV, 1987–2000); *Heartbeat* (ITV, 1992–); *Taggart* (ITV, 1985–); *Sherlock Holmes* (various incarnations, 1984–94), *A Touch of Frost* (ITV, 1992–); *Agatha Christie's Poirot* (BBC, 1989–2002). In 1991, Lynda La Plante's first three-part *Prime Suspect* (ITV) had reinvigorated the genre, exploring the gender politics of policing through Helen Mirren's DCI Jane Tennison, and refocusing the narrative dynamic by introducing its suspect almost from the start, placing the emphasis not on discovering the perpetrator but on the effort to 'make him crack'. *Cracker* would tread both these paths, but its direction was wholly its own.

Cracker straddled two traditions of detective fiction – the collectivist police procedural, typified by *Z Cars* (BBC, 1962–78) and *The Bill*, and the individualist sleuth narrative, exemplified by the literary creations of Christie and Conan Doyle – then for good measure threw in elements of other genres, too, from soap to horror. Fitz made a compelling hero – a prodigiously flawed, wise-cracking smartarse, awesomely arrogant but blessed with the deductive reasoning of Holmes, the cynicism and linguistic gifts of Chandler's Marlowe, the paradigm-leaping intellect of *Twin Peaks*' (US: ABC, 1990–1) Special Agent Dale Cooper (Kyle MacLachlan) – and his pugnacious wit was a powerful antidote to the self-pitying grumpiness of Morse (John Thaw) or Frost (David Jason).

The series' first dazzling episode put to rest any thoughts that this was just another identikit crime drama, beginning with the hero pelting his students with the collected works of Freud, Jung and Spinoza and admitting to fantasies about his father's death, and ending with an acutely disturbing voyage into the dark depths of the human psyche. Coltrane's Fitz knew this grim underworld, and like Dante's Virgil, he was prepared to guide us through it, ready or not. He had looked inside himself, inside all of us, and what he saw was ugly. Rage, murder, rape, he insisted, aren't confined to the fringes of humanity, something *other*; they are part of us, part of the natural order:

3

> Nature knows men have to penetrate women, or the species dies. Now, with all that at stake, do you really think Nature cares how we do it, whether we say please or thank you, whether she's willing? Sex crimes: a little of what Nature requires, taken to excess. Murder too: healthy aggression, taken a little to excess.

Like *Z Cars* before it, *Cracker* fused its detection narrative to a social conscience. Its criminals are manifestations of the state of early 90s Britain, after over a decade of divisive Tory rule, inhabiting a

Manchester riven with unemployment and industrial and economic decay. Theirs are crimes of frustration and rage, the rage of ordinary people driven to the edge by circumstances. They are crimes of human frailty, not venom and malevolent cunning. There are no criminal masterminds here – Fitz's Holmes has no Moriarty (his loss: surely what Fitz wants more than anything is a truly worthy adversary). Crimes of acquisition are absent. So too is the universal scapegoat of drug addiction. Instead, *Cracker*'s perpetrators are fuelled by weakness, hopelessness, desperation, poverty, unendurable grief and deep resentments of the kind that all of us feel to some degree, but most of us manage to control. 'Nobody is born a monster,' Fitz tells us, and they weren't. They differ from us only in the details of their circumstances, and in their inability, under duress, to contain their inner demons. They are *us*, taken 'a little to excess'.

Hillsborough avenger Albie Kinsella (Robert Carlyle) in 'To Be a Somebody', rapist Floyd Malcolm (Graham Aggrey) in 'Men Should Weep', prostitute-killer David Harvey (Mark Lambert) in 'Brotherly Love': each is a phenomenon of modern Britain, but they are more than mere victims of economic and political forces beyond their control. *Cracker* doesn't recoil from blame. These men and women have made choices; their crimes have consequences, have destroyed lives. Theirs are not crimes of resistance, however they might like to rationalise them; those who suffer are not the oppressors.

Cracker's murders are brutal and violent. The series takes us to places where we're uncomfortable to follow, and draws conclusions – about the nature of male sexual desire, or the universality of violent impulses – that we're reluctant to hear. It compels us to look within ourselves, to question and confront our capacity for rage and brutality, to remind ourselves, 'there but for the grace of God . . .'.

Guilt, justice, motive, sacrifice, atonement: *Cracker*'s vocabulary is familiar from law and secular morality. But these words acquire a still greater resonance viewed through the prism of Catholicism. For *Cracker* is a product of its creator Jimmy McGovern's Catholic heritage, which is Fitz's too. It is fuelled, as McGovern puts it, by a 'Catholic conscience'. In his lecture in 'The Mad Woman in the Attic', Fitz follows up his book-throwing theatrics with this 'moral':

> go and lock yourself in a room for a couple of days, and study what is *here*. The things that you *really* feel, not all that crap that you're *supposed* to feel. And when you've studied, when you've shed a little light on the dark recess of your soul, that's the time to pick up a *book*.

To understand human motivation, argues Fitz, look within. This relentless self-examination is at the centre of Catholic doctrine. To purge sin, says the priest, we must first acknowledge and confess it. But that is not enough: we must acknowledge, too, the selfish motives behind our 'good' deeds. We do good because it makes us feel good; there are no pure motives. Fitz is fascinated by Catholicism, however much he professes to hate it. He has lost most of his faith, but this he still believes: there are *no pure motives*. It is this understanding, as much as his training in psychology, that makes Fitz the detective he is.

5

1 The Who, the How and the Why

Part of this book's objective is to make a case for *Cracker*'s consideration as a 'classic' work of television. This has to do with more than a mere statement of quality. I'm not about to argue whether *Cracker* is 'as good as' or 'better than', say, *Cathy Come Home* (BBC, 1966), *Pennies from Heaven* (BBC, 1978), or *Boys from the Blackstuff* (BBC, 1982). Nor am I proposing these as necessarily the best of their respective decades, but they are all works around which a certain critical consensus has gathered to confer classic status. I might just as well have listed *Talking to a Stranger* (BBC, 1966), *The Naked Civil Servant* (Thames for ITV, 1975), *Abigail's Party* (BBC, 1977), *An Englishman Abroad* (BBC, 1983), *Made in Britain* (Central for ITV, 1983) or *Edge of Darkness* (BBC, 1985), all of which have, at one time or another, been described as 'classics'. These programmes share a convergence of popularity and critical praise, high standards of technical achievement and performance, a powerful sense of their time (even if, like *Pennies from Heaven*, they are set in the past). But they are also marked by a confident authorial voice: each is the work of a single writer, working with a sympathetic director and producer; even though *Cathy Come Home* is today more closely associated with its director (Ken Loach) than with its writer (Jeremy Sandford), this was not so completely the case at the time.

Another common feature of the above list is that all were produced before the end of the 1980s. There is as yet little consensus about what, if anything, constitutes classic television after that time. Indeed, much of the critical comment on contemporary television prefers to see mostly a decline in standards, a generalised retreat from the 'golden age' of television in the 1960s and 70s, brought about by an increasingly commercial, risk-averse broadcasting culture (see, for example, Day-Lewis, 1998), particularly in the ITV that emerged after the franchise auction heralded by the 1990 Broadcasting Act. In this analysis, contemporary television tirelessly reproduces and repackages a number of carefully worked formulae to satisfy diverse audience tastes, while innovative, individual and, especially, politically engaged work is marginalised.

This aggressively commercialised new broadcasting climate, marked in the 1990s by the centralisation of commissioning in John Birt's BBC and by an ITV heavily reliant on established star vehicles for the likes of John Thaw or David Jason, is typically characterised as hostile to writers. As Lez Cooke notes,

> the writer with an 'authorial vision' was now considered to be a luxury that most television companies could no longer afford . . . what was required in the market-driven context of the 1990s were writers who could develop marketable projects which would win and retain audiences. Indeed the concept to be developed might not be an original idea brought to a producer by a writer but a concept developed by TV drama commissioners, perhaps in collaboration with a writer who might then be invited to develop the idea if it was deemed potentially marketable. (Cooke, 2003: 164)

This might well be a regrettable trend, but the case of *Cracker* – which fits this development pattern almost exactly – shows that it doesn't inevitably lead to safe or predictable programming, nor to a stifling of the writer's voice.

When ITV found itself facing the temporary (as it turned out) retirement of its cash-cow *Inspector Morse*, the call went out for a detective drama to plug the gap. In response to a circular from Sally Head, Granada's head of drama, for commissioning ideas, producer

Gub Neal hastily drew up an outline, based on an idea he had been mulling over since his brief time as a producer on *Prime Suspect 2*. His conception was not of a sedate, crossword-solving copper in the Morse mould, but of a 'totally new-age detective'. A trained criminal psychologist, rather than a policeman or a genteel amateur sleuth, he was 'working-class, but an academic', using

> anthropology, animal psychology, but mainly his own mind as a drawing board for penetrating crime. . . . The town marshal with a pocket full of Jung. He uncovers the mysteries behind the criminal mind. . . .
> The question for this man starts not with who but why. (Crace, 1995: 14)

At this stage, the character was called Jonas. It was only now that Neal first approached a writer.

Personality may be a key factor here: Neal had already established a reputation as a producer who encouraged innovative

8

Gub Neal

drama. But the fact remains that *Cracker* not only appeared in the middle of television drama's perceived decline but emerged from precisely the commissioning climate that was held largely responsible for it. And although the call was for a substitute for the stately *Morse*, what resulted was not more of the same but a drama, as Neal puts it, 'as noisy and as angry and as difficult and as awkward and as complex as we could have dreamed' (Neal, 2007). And, he might have added, as *authored*.

Two of the most commonly cited expressions – or causes – of TV drama's malaise are the disappearance of the single play and the increased prevalence of soap opera and, more especially, its invasion of other genres, from drama series to documentary. The writers who had dominated 'serious' television drama in the 1960s, 70s and 80s – figures like John Hopkins, John McGrath, Dennis Potter, Alan Plater, Troy Kennedy Martin, Trevor Griffiths, Alan Bennett, David Mercer – had all been significant contributors to high-profile, high-status single drama anthologies like ITV's *Armchair Theatre* (1956–74) or *Playhouse* (1967–83), or the BBC's *The Wednesday Play* (1964–70) or *Play for Today* (1970–84). Some strands, like the thirty-minute *Teletales* (BBC, 1963–4), were specifically created to introduce writers new to television. The single drama was, if not necessarily an apprenticeship, then something like a 'sandpit': a space where writers could experiment, develop their craft, find their 'voice'.

But by the mid-1980s the main single drama strands had come to a close, leaving only a few isolated slots. And while Channel 4's *Film on Four* and the BBC's later *Screen One* and *Screen Two* might fill a similar slot in the schedules as *Play for Today* and its kin once had, their feature-film production values and consequently higher cost meant that producers were much less inclined to look to inexperienced writers for their scripts. Dennis Potter, for one, looking back on his career shortly before his death, worried how new writers could possibly develop in such an inhospitable climate: 'I was given the space to grow into . . . . Whereas if I was starting now, where would I get that chance? Who would cosset and look after me? Where is the single play?' (Potter, 1984: 16).

Writers arriving in television from the early 1980s on had to look elsewhere for their opportunities. Increasingly, they came not in anthology dramas but in more populist forms: children's television and, especially, soap opera. It's striking just how many of today's most conspicuous television writers learned their craft in one or both of these: Russell T. Davies cut his teeth on kids' series like *Why Don't You . . .?* (BBC, 1973–95) and *Children's Ward/The Ward* (ITV, 1989–2001); Paula Milne on soaps *Crossroads* (ITV, 1966–88) and *Coronation Street* (ITV, 1960–); Kay Mellor on *Coronation Street* and *Brookside* (Channel 4, 1982–2003). Even Andrew Davies, old enough to number a *Wednesday Play* among his early credits, wrote numerous items for children's variety show *Little Big Time* (ITV, 1968), and created the anarchic children's hit *Educating Marmalade* (ITV, 1982–3). Any list of the best of contemporary British TV writers would surely include most or all of these names, though two are missing: Jimmy McGovern, writer of seven *Cracker* stories, and Paul Abbott, writer of three. They too have their roots in soap: McGovern in *Brookside* and Abbott in *Coronation Street* (Abbott also developed *Children's Ward* with Kay Mellor).

It may be true that writers are, as Dennis Potter worried, less 'cosseted' today than they once were. But some writers *have* thrived without the opportunities afforded by the single play, and it may even be that the more ratings-driven demands of continuing series and soaps offer their own opportunities for some who might, early in their careers, have struggled to get commissions for authored works.
Jimmy McGovern, for one, is supremely grateful for his *Brookside* apprenticeship: 'I wouldn't have got near a *Wednesday Play* because I wasn't good enough. I didn't know enough . . . . I think that high volume of churning stuff out [on *Brookside*], it really worked for me, it really taught me' (McGovern, 2007a).

Brought on board by *Brookside* creator Phil Redmond as part of a commitment to foster local talent, McGovern started on episode 14 (broadcast December 1982), and stayed on until episode 704 (July 1989), contributing nearly 90 episodes. In the absence of the single play,

Jimmy McGovern

soap, as represented by *Brookside* and, later, *EastEnders* (BBC, 1985–), was repositioned, at least for a time, as the most immediate TV form for the transmission of social and political anxieties. McGovern was a driving force during *Brookside*'s most politically engaged period, when characters like Ricky Tomlinson's Bobby Grant and John McArdle's Billy Corkhill experienced life at the sharp end of Thatcherism. 'I can have far more effect as regards the bringing forward of an alternative society than left-wing playwright Howard Brenton could ever have,' he told the *Guardian* in 1986 (Willis, 1986).

Paul Abbott

In Bobby Grant, particularly, McGovern found a character
through which he could act out his frustrations about what he saw as a
new victimisation of the white working class. Bobby was a socialist, an
active trade unionist, a Catholic, a father of three: his biography was
strikingly similar to McGovern's own. As *Brookside* developed, Bobby
came to see all he believed in under assault: the hard rightward swing of
80s politics saw not only the frustration of his own political dreams, but
an all-out assault on the trade unions that represented to him working-
class political expression and strength. At the same time, his class
alienated him from a political constituency that he had considered his
own. In the eyes of the middle-class left, he was assumed to embody a
host of outdated, sexist, racist attitudes, while his inability to master the
language of leftist political discourse saw him treated with scorn by
those he had assumed would be his allies. Meanwhile, his fruitless
devotion to his causes saw a rift open up between him and his family,

and when his wife, Sheila (Sue Johnston) was raped, Bobby – a compassionate man, but a traditional one – found himself well out of his emotional depth, unable to find in himself the strength to give her the full support she demanded.

McGovern's growing disillusion with the left came to a head at the end of the 1980s. Not with the fall of the Berlin Wall and its symbolic enactment of the toppling of Communism, but in a more local event of at least, for the writer, equivalent symbolic importance. On 15 April 1989, ninety-four Liverpool football supporters lost their lives (the total ultimately reached ninety-six) at Sheffield's Hillsborough stadium, where Liverpool were scheduled to play Nottingham Forest in an FA Cup semi-final, when a combination of inadequate safety procedures and defective crowd management led to horrific overcrowding on the terraces.

The crush at the stadium's Leppings Lane end followed the decision by the senior police officer, Chief Superintendent Duckenfield, to open a locked gate in order to relieve pressure building up outside the ground. The tragic result was a far worse crush inside: without any stewards or police to steer the new arrivals into the outer 'pens' – where there was still plenty of standing space – they were driven into the already overfull central pens. Attempts by those at the front to escape the crush by scaling the perimeter fencing were initially interpreted by the police as a pitch invasion, and officers were dispatched to push them back.

As the dust settled, Duckenfield, rather than admit his own culpability, claimed that Liverpool fans had forced the fatal gate. Upon this mendacious foundation was built the edifice of distortion and myth that characterised early accounts of the tragedy and proved stubbornly hard to shift: Liverpool fans had been drinking unusually heavily; the crush was caused by fans arriving late and determined to get in at all costs; many had turned up without tickets. This line, aggressively pushed by the South Yorkshire police, was reported, mostly uncritically, in the press and television news.

The first official report into the disaster, by Lord Justice Taylor, offered some solace to the grieving families of the Hillsborough dead.

13

While criticising safety standards at Hillsborough, and noting ruefully the extent to which the control of a small minority of hooligans had superseded the welfare of ordinary, decent spectators as the priority of clubs, police and politicians alike, Taylor dismissed the suggestion that drunken and ticketless fans were a major contributor, and put the blame firmly on the South Yorkshire Police, concluding that 'the main reason for the disaster was the failure of police control' (Taylor, 1989: para 278).

Encouraged by Taylor's damning judgment, the families expected that justice would now take its course. But in the face of sustained police pressure, the process began to turn against them. The Coroner's Inquest recorded a verdict not of 'unlawful killing', but of 'accidental death'. The Director of Public Prosecutions rejected charges against South Yorkshire officers; the independent Police Complaints Authority felt differently, but was forced to drop its charges when Duckenfield retired early on health grounds. The families were left with minimal compensation (while police victims of trauma got much more), bereft and furious at what seemed a monstrous travesty of justice. Much of Liverpool shared their anger and bitterness. For McGovern, the disaster would mark the final extinguishing of the faith in the ideologies of the left that he had been wrestling with throughout the 1980s; Hillsborough seemed, in retrospect, the consequence not only of police incompetence but of the left's abject abandonment of the white working class. The outpouring of grief and the sense of burning injustice of Hillsborough would fuel *Cracker* and, later, the drama-documentary *Hillsborough* (ITV, 1996), but its more immediate impact surfaced in his relationship with his *Brookside* mentor, Phil Redmond.

The rift with Redmond began when a producer cut a scene McGovern had written in which a character burned copies of *The Sun*, in protest against that paper's slanderous allegations a few days after the disaster that Liverpool fans had robbed and even urinated on the dead.[1] McGovern was incensed at the cut, and when Redmond backed his producer, McGovern saw this as evidence that the programme had lost its political backbone; he left not long after (Day-Lewis, 1998).

While *Brookside* had nurtured McGovern's talents, he found it harder to sell his ideas elsewhere: 'I wasn't trusted by anybody. I was nothing but a soap-opera writer' (McGovern, in Butler (1995)). In 1992, with three single dramas to add to his CV, including the well-received *Needle* (BBC, 1990), he was still struggling to get the BBC to produce his ambitious multi-part drama, *Priest*, the project he'd been nursing for the best part of a decade. There's no little irony in the fact that it was Michael Wearing – who had supported *Boys from the Blackstuff* in the face of opposition from senior BBC executives, and who was long considered a steadfast champion of writers – who ultimately turned *Priest* down.

Enter Gub Neal. Neal had none of the disdain for soap writers that McGovern had encountered elsewhere. His own entry into television had come in the mid-1980s, on the production team of *EastEnders*, and his credits as producer included the post-watershed serial *Medics* (ITV, 1990–5), created by the same partnership, Julia Smith and Tony Holland, behind *EastEnders*. Neal had seen and admired *Needle*, and he wanted McGovern for *Cracker*, persevering even while the writer was still attached to the BBC on *Priest*.

But with *Priest* apparently in oblivion (the drama was ultimately rewritten as a TV film, released theatrically in 1994 and broadcast in BBC2's *Screen Two* slot in 1995), McGovern seized on *Cracker* as a lifeline. Neal remembers the first script coming in record time, and more than meeting his expectations: 'I got this 100-page script, that had clearly slid on to the page with extraordinary veracity and bite … it read like a firework' (Neal, 2007). In fact, McGovern was using *Cracker* as a kind of primal scream therapy – to express his pent-up anger, 'post-Hillsborough, the assault upon the white working-class male, the '80s', but, most of all, he admits, to vent his anger over *Priest*. 'I actually turned over *Priest* and started writing,' he recalls, 'I wrote *Cracker* on the back of my rejected *Priest*, fuelled with rage, that burning sense of anger about the way the BBC had treated me' (McGovern, 2007a).

Anger has always been a crucial element of McGovern's writing, for reasons beyond temperament and politics. Born in

15

Liverpool to working-class parents in 1949, he was the fifth of nine children. Perhaps the constant hubbub of a large family was overwhelming, but for whatever reason, the young Jimmy communicated only in more-or-less wordless sounds, somehow interpreted for the rest of the family by his brother Joey, two years his senior. Even when, at around eight or nine, he began to speak in intelligible sentences, he suffered a crippling stammer. Mostly, with Joey's help and his family's patience, he 'got by', but the stammer was at its most disabling when it came to the rituals he was expected to participate in at church. The certainty that the stains on his soul could only be washed clean by confession made the regular Sacrament of Penance a torture for a tongue-tied young believer. If he should die before he confessed his sins, he knew, he would surely go to Hell. But his anxiety only made more acute his inability to form the words (McGovern, 2007a). This private torment is powerfully evoked in McGovern's 2000 BBC film, *Liam*.

Two things, the boy Jimmy discovered, could bring order to his disjointed speech. If he gave the words rhythm or melody, he could get them out without the agony. This revelation led the adult McGovern to theorise that his affliction was a consequence of his family's departure from Ireland in the mid-nineteenth century. Even generations on, he feels, he is paying the penalty for having been severed from the songlike rhythms of his forefathers' speech (McGovern, 2007a). While talking in rhythm (or in the slow, drawn way that speech therapy taught him) helped his words to take shape, speaking like this felt and sounded stilted, unnatural. When roused to anger, though, he found the fluency that had eluded him. With no self-consciousness interrupting the flow from thought to enunciation, the words came out easily.

It's not hard to imagine why writing should come to appeal. If he couldn't speak the words himself (though his impediment became less severe in adulthood, he still stammers a little even today), his characters could speak them for him. And his childhood discoveries – the urgency of communication and, especially, honesty before God (because, as the Church told him, the future of his soul depended on it), the release that anger could bring – were translated into his written prose. Much of McGovern's passion and vibrancy, his fierce honesty as a writer, surely comes from here. And his understanding of human motivation, derived from the ceaseless self-questioning that the Church had demanded of him, the realisation that what he had felt others had too, was put to a new use, giving his characters depth, intensity and a moral complexity that took them off the page and into the real world.

It was McGovern who fleshed out the concept of *Cracker*, but the title was Neal's – inspired, he says, by a packet of cream crackers in a shop window. He was struck by the word's versatility and resonance, which was more than confirmed when he later consulted a dictionary. Most obviously, a cracker is one who breaks apart or into something (as in a 'safe-cracker'), or breaks someone down ('I'll make him crack'); one who solves a puzzle, riddle or mystery (a detective, of course, 'cracks a case'). It has connotations of noise and flash ('crack a whip', 'pistol-crack', 'crack of thunder', 'fire-cracker'); of excellence or pre-eminence ('a crack shot'); of madness or mental instability ('cracked', 'crackers'); of damage or flaw; of haste or urgency ('crack on', 'get cracking'). It can suggest a bold attempt ('have a crack at'), or a joke or cutting remark ('wisecrack'). The OED also offers 'a boaster, a braggart; hence, a liar'. There is also the potent and addictive drug derived from cocaine, and the implied 'nutcracker': 'nut', of course, being slang for both a mad person and the head – thus someone who 'cracks open heads'. Finally, in reference to one of Fitz's less endearing habits, there's also the slang 'to crack', meaning to break wind. It seemed a richly appropriate title, more enigmatic and intriguing than the obvious 'Fitz'.[2]

There would be no theme music, no title sequence. This meant sacrificing the iconic impact that had helped a series like *Callan* (ITV, 1967–72) – whose outsider hero was an early inspiration for Neal in his original outline (Neal, 2007) – with its slow, reverbed bass guitar and swinging lightbulb illuminating a rough brick wall. But it would give *Cracker*'s directors greater freedom to determine the look and feel of each story. The title would appear in plain white text on a stark black background (as *Prime Suspect*'s had done) and the music – if there was

17

music – would be selected by the director, though the dominant theme was inflected by jazz and piano blues, to suit McGovern's conception of Fitz's own tastes.

Granada had taken a publicity photograph of Fitz – full length, colour, in his dark-blue suit. Neal hated it: it was Coltrane the comedian, not Fitz. He preferred the hunched, head-and-shoulders shot, in chiaroscuro black and white, grim-faced, dark eyes probing and cigarette smoke spiralling over his shoulder – the Fitz you would cower from in the interrogation room. This became the image that sandwiched

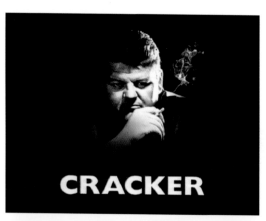

An echo of TV past: Fitz and *The Human Jungle*'s Dr Corder (Herbert Lom)

the advert breaks, and gave *Cracker* a memorable visual identity in lieu of a title sequence. It was moody, unsettling, *noir*-ish: Fitz as he might have liked to see himself, in a 1940s Hollywood movie starring Bogart or Cagney. Deliberately or otherwise, it also recalled, for those with long memories, an image from British television's distant past – Herbert Lom's psychiatrist, Dr Roger Corder, half-obscured in shadows and entwined in his own cigarette smoke, in the titles of *The Human Jungle* (ITV, 1963–5).

McGovern was determined not to fall back, as he had seen other writers do, on the clichés, the stock plots and characters, all the comfortable, predictable elements familiar from a hundred other crime series:

> A crime drama is the easiest thing in the world to write . . . . You've got your in-built structure: motivation, perpetration, discovery of crime, investigation, interrogation. It is so easy. And therefore, in the midst of that crime story, you are duty-bound . . . to say something meaningful about life. (McGovern, 1995)

19

He was happy to retain this structure: *Cracker* stories invariably ran through the list, though motivation tended to be fully revealed only towards the end. The difference lay in the balance of the component parts. With the perpetrator generally revealed at the beginning – it was 'how' and 'why' that interested McGovern and Neal, not 'who' – the narrative strategy was concerned less with sharing clues with the audience to draw them into the enigma than with bringing forward the inevitable and hotly anticipated climactic encounter with Fitz.

The interrogation scenes, not the pursuit, the capture or even the crime itself, were *Cracker*'s dramatic epicentre. It was counterintuitive that this should work as television drama. A single, almost bare room, in which two characters engaged in an intellectual arm-wrestle for several minutes at a time: this was *theatre*. Where was the *action*? The various directors devoted much energy to their set-ups for these scenes: employing long takes, elaborate pans, slow zooms, focus pulls, extreme close-ups; changing angles frequently, moving the actors around the set. But their best assets were the intensity of McGovern's dialogue and the sheer attack of Coltrane's performance, which inspired the other actors to raise their own to match it. With guest stars of the calibre of Robert Carlyle, David Calder, Christopher Fulford, Susan Lynch, Jim Carter and Liam Cunningham, there was something gladiatorial about these confrontations. As Fitz and his opponents faced off, you could see the sparks.

McGovern poured himself into Fitz: his gambling, his drinking, his grievances against Catholicism, all of his anger and self-loathing . . . even his birthday (the same day as Twiggy, jokes Fitz). Just as the writer channelled a lifetime's examination of his conscience into penetrating the psychological and emotional worlds of his characters, so Fitz would apply the same techniques to understanding the criminal mind. And McGovern poured himself, too, into *Cracker*'s perpetrators: Sean (Andrew Tiernan) in 'To Say I Love You' got his stammer and his volatility; Albie in 'To Be a Somebody' got his rage at Hillsborough and the vilification of the white working class; the gift of all his darkest old prejudices – and his first name – he bestowed on the bubbling cauldron that was DS Jimmy Beck (Lorcan Cranitch).

Though not all of *Cracker*'s perpetrators were male, a major element of the series – including the stories written by Ted Whitehead and Paul Abbott – was the examination of masculinity *in extremis*, of men wrestling with their new status in a world where old certainties about traditional masculine 'strengths' were being questioned. These changes were, by the early 1990s, increasingly being expressed in the very form of television drama. Christine Gledhill, responding to the increasing incursion of what was once seen as an essentially female dramatic mode into previously 'male' strongholds like the police genre, noted: 'for soap opera structures to operate inside a "male" genre, a break is required with conventions of gender representation – which dictate taciturnity and invincibility as marks of masculinity and construe talk about personal feelings as "feminizing"' (Gledhill, 1992: 119).

Perhaps incidentally, *Cracker* found for itself an almost perfect mechanism for effecting just such a break. By the device of having a psychologist at its centre, and by making him, rather than the police, the chief interrogator, it creates the conditions in which its male perpetrators are able – or obliged – to open up about their 'personal feelings', encouraged or coerced by Fitz to attempt to explain and understand what may appear the most violent and unintelligible acts.

The 1980s and 90s saw a creeping incursion of soap attributes into other television genres. One notable example of this trend was *The Bill*'s 1987 shift from a single sixty-minute slot to two (later three) thirty-minute slots per week. But a more likely influence on McGovern's *Cracker* were the US serials *Hill Street Blues* (NBC, 1981–7) and, especially, *Twin Peaks*, former *Hill Street* writer Mark Frost and David Lynch's ambitious fusion of detective fiction, police procedural, soap opera, horror and comedy with Lynch's signature metaphysics. While *Cracker* is content to remain on the terrestrial plane, it borrows freely from all of these genres, as we shall see. And Fitz has much in common with *Twin Peaks*' Special Agent Cooper: both arrive as outsiders to a police investigation (though *Twin Peaks*' police force is altogether more benevolent than *Cracker*'s), bringing skills and insights that frequently bamboozle their more down-to-earth associates, while Fitz's Catholic understanding of motive has its (albeit inexact) counterpart in Cooper's 'Tibetan method'. McGovern has acknowledged a debt to *Twin Peaks* for at least one scene in 'To Say I Love You', while the retrieval of the plastic-wrapped body from the lake in 'Mad Woman' recalls the discovery of Laura Palmer's (Sheryl Lee) body that kicks off *Twin Peaks* (Ted Whitehead's *Cracker* story, 'The Big Crunch', goes much further in its homage). The Frost/Lynch series, too, predates *Cracker*'s recognition of the dramatic impact of grief, as its early episodes survey the effect of Laura's death on her small-town community in general and her parents in particular.

Soap's most obvious distinguishing characteristics, its serial structure and its eternal suspension of narrative resolution, are reflected not only in *Cracker*'s distinctive semi-serial form (three more or less

21

distinct multi-episode stories per series), but also in the manifold subplots, from the Fitz–Judith rollercoaster and the parallel twists of Fitz's seduction of DS Penhaligon (Geraldine Somerville) to his relationships with his children Mark (Kieran O'Brien) and Katie (Tess Thomson), which permeate the borders of the individual stories. The events of DCI Bilborough's (Christopher Eccleston) marriage – wife Catriona's (Amelia Bullmore/Isobel Middleton) pregnancy, the arrival of baby Ryan (Ryan Cooper), Bilborough's death and Catriona's attempts to come to terms with it – are another strand that weaves between episodes, as are DS Beck's personal crisis following Bilborough's death, his rape of Penhaligon and his efforts to assuage his guilt by offering support to Catriona, while clearly entertaining hopes of a relationship with her (hopes that are dashed, in a very soap-ish melodramatic device, by the revelation that Catriona has taken up with her dead husband's brother).

McGovern's final two stories unfold almost as one, sharing similar themes (male violence against women; entrenched misogyny in the police force) and bridged by another favourite soap device, the cliffhanger. Although the two stories are separated by some four months in narrative time, Penhaligon's rape by Beck in 'Men Should Weep' is resolved in 'Brotherly Love' (and its ripples continue into Paul Abbott's first story, 'Best Boys'), just as the revelation of Judith's pregnancy in the first story is followed by the baby's delivery in the second (while 'Best Boys' explores Judith's subsequent isolation and postnatal depression). The arrival of Fitz's brother Danny (Clive Russell) in 'Brotherly Love' begins another plotline, following his growing closeness to Judith, which runs into 'True Romance' two stories later.

Prime Suspect's nine stories collectively offer up two funerals. *Cracker*'s eleven stories, by contrast, contain three funerals, three weddings, two births and one christening. This preponderance echoes the 'big events' by which soaps periodically boost audience excitement. *Cracker*'s big events come without the media fanfare typical of the soaps', but share their tendency to use them for major dramatic revelation (Geraghty, 1991). The sparsely attended funeral of Albie's father in 'To Be a Somebody' is the catalyst for his killing spree;

Fitz's mother's funeral in 'Brotherly Love' is the occasion for new insights into his relationships with his family and his detachment from his working-class past; Beck's funeral in 'Best Boys' shows us how Penhaligon is coping with his death. And just as *Coronation Street* might undercut the solemnity of a funeral with humour, so 'Brotherly Love' gives us the daft spectacle of a game of bingo in honour of the late Mrs Fitzgerald. In 'True Romance', the wedding of Nena (Fleur Bennett) alerts us to the existence of a shocking family secret (although its revelation comes much later), while indicating her sister Janice's (Emily Joyce) manipulative neurosis.

The adoption of soap-style storytelling came naturally to McGovern and Abbott by virtue of their respective backgrounds. But their directors, too, were largely free of old prejudices against the genre. Of *Cracker*'s ten directors, all but one – Roy Battersby – had entered the industry in the 1980s or 90s, and five had served time on soaps: Tim Fywell and Richard Standeven on *Brookside*, Julian Jarrold on *Coronation Street*, Jean Stewart and Antonia Bird on *EastEnders*. Most of the remainder had directed episodes of ongoing popular dramas – *Casualty* (BBC, 1986–) (Charles McDougall), *The Bill* (Standeven, Stewart) and, especially, the Gub Neal-produced *Medics* (Standeven, Stewart, Simon Cellan Jones). Andy Wilson had taken another very 1980s route into television by directing pop videos, while even Michael Winterbottom – ultimately the most successful of the group – who unusually had already directed some standalone dramas, had also contributed to the children's anthology series *Dramarama* (ITV, 1983).

Cracker, then, was overwhelmingly the work of a generation of writers, producers and directors (and even actors) that had entered the medium when the 'golden age' of 'classic television' was, according to conventional wisdom, dead or dying. And yet its continuing popular and critical respect, and the fact that it has lost none of its power to shock and disturb, despite more explicitly gruesome drama since (most obviously, *Messiah* (BBC, 2001–)) are strong arguments for its acknowledgment as a classic in its own right.

To an extent, it is a status that the series has already earned for itself. In the BFI's *TV100*, a 2000 poll of industry figures across six

23

Weddings,
births, funerals:
'True Romance'

'Brotherly Love'

'To Be a
Somebody'

'Cracker'
(2006 special)

'One Day a
Lemming Will
Fly'

25

'Brotherly Love'

genres, *Cracker* came in at number nine in the drama series and serials category and thirty-ninth in the overall list. When Channel 4 polled another group of insiders seven years later for its *50 Greatest TV Dramas* (2007), *Cracker* managed eighth place in a list that included not only single dramas like *Cathy Come Home* but also American TV.

In its lifetime, though, *Cracker* occupied a more ambiguous position. Press reviews for the first story, 'The Mad Woman in the Attic' were almost uniformly glowing, generously dividing praise between lead actor, director and writer. It was 'an original and highly entertaining thriller,' with 'taut writing, plenty of tension, some wry humour and sharp characterisation' (*Daily Mail*); 'as exciting a debut as you could hope to see' (*Evening Standard*); Jaci Stephen in the *New Statesman & Society* praised 'McGovern's intense and gripping script', 'Michael Winterbottom's superb direction,' and 'Coltrane's ability to bring both mania and gentleness to the part'. The *Independent*'s Thomas Sutcliffe – McGovern's own pick of the broadsheet critics (Day-Lewis, 1998) – posted the most perceptive review, noting that 'after a decade of judicial miscarriages, it's hardly surprising that the whodunnit should have given way to the didhedoit,' marvelling at the 'casual veracity' of the writing, and celebrating 'a whole range of pleasures from brisk procedural ... to a sense of lives extending beyond the frame of the story'. Only the *Guardian*'s Hugh Hebert sounded a more cautious note, acknowledging the 'deadpan comic boldness', but arguing, idiosyncratically, that 'characters who ditch their first names are suspect'.

But while the review pages may have been (initially) in favour, the news and opinion pages of the rightwing press were more hostile. With debates raging about the perceived excess of violence and sex on television, *Cracker* was held up as another example of the medium 'pushing at the boundaries of taste and decency'. The Broadcasting Standards Council (the entirely superfluous 'watchdog' that essentially duplicated the regulatory functions of the Independent Television Commission and the BBC Governors, but whose judgments, frequently based on just one or two green-inked complaints, were routinely reported in the pages of the *Mail*, *Telegraph* and others) received a small handful of complaints about each of the stories in the original three-series run, upholding or partly upholding most of them. Typical was its conclusion that the scenes of the murdered body in the train in 'Mad Woman' were 'too protracted and unnecessarily graphic'.

In October 1994, following the stabbing to death of a forty-year-old midwife in her home, a Lincolnshire coroner let it be known that he felt it 'a considerable coincidence' that the murder came 'just twelve hours' after a *Cracker* story (the Hillsborough-themed 'To Be a Somebody') featuring two stabbings. Despite offering no evidence of any direct connection or of further similarities, he was widely quoted. The same story brought a more predictable outcry from the South Yorkshire police, whose Chief Constable Richard Wells wrote to (then producer) Paul Abbott to express his 'concern and sadness' about the Hillsborough storyline, having received a 'flurry' of calls from distressed officers present at the tragedy. In an article in the *Daily Mirror* on 27 October, Wells acknowledged that 'the fans and the families are still hurting,' but insisted, 'so too are my officers'. McGovern, interviewed in the same paper a month later, wryly noted that the attacks had come from the two professions who had most profoundly failed the Hillsborough families – the police and the coroners.

Thereafter, press outrage gathered pace. The opening scene of 'The Big Crunch', featuring a headmaster having open-air sex with a pupil, drew condemnation from the previously unknown Community Standards Association, whose spokeswoman worried, bizarrely, that 'young girls who saw this sleazy programme could be terrified of their teachers now' (*Daily Record*, 2 November 1994).

The *Daily Star* reported a 'furious backlash' after 'Brotherly Love' offered up 'some of the most sickening sex and violence ever seen on British TV' (23 October 1995). The *Daily Express* judged *Cracker* 'incredibly good quality drama,' but complained, 'the violence and downright seediness . . . has become repulsive' (25 October 1995).

Perhaps cowed by the condemnation on the news pages, some of the critics began to step back from the earlier rapture. Reviewing 'To Be a Somebody', Matthew Bond, in *The Times*, lamented the

'Tarantino-like approach to blood and gore,' while the *Daily Mail*'s Peter Paterson complained that '*Cracker* has conned us down a path of sleaze, immorality, corruption and filth.'

Audiences, as it turned out, were rather more loyal. From a respectable but not earth-shattering start – hovering between 9.8 and 10.1 million viewers each for the first four episodes (according to the BARB ratings) – numbers began to climb. By the end of its first series *Cracker* was nestling just behind popular drama's leading pack (*Casualty*, *Heartbeat*, *London's Burning* (LWT, 1988) and *Soldier, Soldier* (ITV, 1991–7)) with nearly 12 million viewers. By the end of the second it was in the top three with 15.2 million (equal to *Prime Suspect*'s 1993 high-water mark), a total bested by the numbers tuning in for 'Brotherly Love', which averaged 15.7 million an episode.

For McGovern, still sore with the BBC over *Priest*, success was the best revenge – 'The BBC put everything against *Cracker* for three years, and we wiped the floor' (McGovern, 2007a). Even *Panorama*'s must-watch interview with Princess Diana (BBC, 3 December 1995) failed to make much of a dent: the first part of Abbott's 'True Romance' still managed 12.4 million.

Nor did the media feeding frenzy bother the industry too much. The series' three-year span saw Granada's trophy cabinet fill up: *Cracker* received 14 BAFTA nominations between 1994 and 1996, winning seven, including three consecutive best actor awards for Robbie Coltrane, and back-to-back best drama series awards in 1995 and 1996. McGovern, meanwhile, won the Dennis Potter award for best television dramatist in 1995, and was honoured at the 1996 Writers' Guild Awards as creator of the best original drama series. Coltrane also picked up the Silver Nymph award at the 1994 Monte Carlo Television Awards and the best actor gong at the 1995 Royal Television Society Awards.

Neither audience nor accolades are enough to confirm *Cracker*'s 'classic-ness'. The history of television is littered with works which were celebrated in their time before disappearing into obscurity. *Cracker* hasn't faded yet, and it's notable that ITV's resurrection of the series in 2006, alongside *Prime Suspect*, came at a point when the channel was in profound need of a critical and ratings hit. But ultimately the survival of *Cracker* in the public imagination rests on the durability of its themes, stories and characters, which, notwithstanding their engagement with their own place and time, remain as alive today as they were in the early 1990s.

2 The Shape of Fitz

At the centre of *Cracker* stands Fitz: psychologist, detective, husband, father, gambler, drinker, chain-smoker and, as embodied by Robbie Coltrane, one of the most compelling television figures of the 1990s. It is Fitz who gives us our introduction to *Cracker*'s crimes and criminals, and we view them through the lens of his piercing intellect.

Jimmy McGovern originally conceived of his hero as 'a thin, wiry man with a sense of danger – a John Cassavetes type' (Crace, 1995: 15) – not unlike himself. Gub Neal considered Robert Lindsay, having admired the actor's nervy performance in Alan Bleasdale's *G.B.H.* (Channel 4, 1991). But to the relief of McGovern (who isn't a fan), Lindsay ultimately turned down the role. Another early candidate was the thin, wiry and dangerous Keith Allen (the suggestion of Danny Boyle, who was at one point lined up to direct). Arguably the edgiest, least house-trained performer of the early-80s alternative comedy generation, Allen might have brought a fierce energy to the role and, when sporting a beard, he can bear a more than passing physical resemblance to Jimmy McGovern, making him an intriguing choice for the writer's *alter ego*. Casting a McGovern *doppelgänger* might, however, have overstressed the autobiographical elements of the character, allowing less space for Fitz to grow as a distinct individual. Most importantly, though, it's hard to imagine a Keith Allen Fitz resonating with audiences in the way that Coltrane's did.

It tends to be mistily remembered that, before *Cracker*, Coltrane was essentially a comic actor, but in fact his appearances in

Alfresco (ITV, 1982), and *The Comic Strip Presents* ... (BBC, 1982) had long coexisted with 'serious' roles for the likes of Lindsay Anderson (*Britannia Hospital*, 1982), Neil Jordan (*Mona Lisa*, 1986) and Derek Jarman (*Carravaggio*, 1986). Coltrane's unruly, self-destructive rock 'n' roller Danny McGlone in John Byrne's blackly comic *Tutti Frutti* (BBC, 1987) appears in retrospect an early prototype for Fitz, and Danny's relationship with the skinny, ditsy Suzi Kettles (Emma Thompson) anticipates Fitz's similarly mismatched romance with DS Penhaligon. But it was Coltrane's performance in the *Screen One* black comedy 'Alive and Kicking' (BBC, 1991) that particularly impressed Neal. An unorthodox drugs counsellor trying to save dealer and junkie Lenny Henry from himself, Coltrane's Liam Kane had many Fitz-like attributes: a sardonic wit, an alcoholic past and a prickly exterior concealing an empathetic core.

McGovern recognised that Coltrane's charisma could help to win sympathy for a character he feared might be too unlikeable, but he was still wedded to his own mental image of Fitz, and in a drunken lunch with the actor and Gub Neal, seemed intent on putting Coltrane off. Thankfully, Neal won, and McGovern, chastened by the verdict of history, vowed never again to dispute a casting decision.

For all McGovern's misgivings, a bulky Fitz perhaps better fits the logic of the character. Fitz is, after all, a man of appetites: for the thrill of risk, for alcohol, for cigarettes, for sex, for intellectual challenge, for experience. And Coltrane's sheer physical size makes him an intimidating presence when he goes head to head with *Cracker*'s more formidable characters. Added to this is his accent: when it comes to indicators of 'hardness', Coltrane's Glaswegian arguably puts Fitz top of the league, above even Mancunian and Scouse.[3] And more importantly, it makes him convincingly Celtic, an asset when the character is so crucially a lapsed Catholic.

While the casting of Coltrane showed audacity, *Cracker*'s most obvious departure from crime genre norms was the decision to make its hero neither a policeman nor an amateur detective, but a criminal psychologist. This was a genuine innovation in British television, and it

The many
aspects of Fitz:
the husband

The teacher

The lover

The interrogator

The father

33

The gambler

allowed the series to explore territory untouched by previous crime series. Fitz's most obvious fictional antecedent is the psychiatrist/profiler-turned-serial killer Hannibal Lecter, created by the novelist Thomas Harris and incarnated most successfully on screen by Anthony Hopkins in *The Silence of the Lambs* (1990). While the 'slasher' cycle of the 1980s presented its killers as, essentially, a malevolent (super)natural force, killing machines with no interior lives and little or no discernible motive, *The Silence of the Lambs* explored the psychological make-up of its killer, establishing convincing goals, behavioural patterns and formative experiences. Lecter himself was a fascinating character, by turns charming and chilling, combining a genius-level intellect and sophisticated cultural tastes with an appetite for staggering violence, cruelty and debauchery. His example recalibrated the genre, creating a new cultural vogue for screen serial killers who were more recognisably human, more psychologically sophisticated (though no less evil) than their typically masked counterparts of the previous decade.

But while Fitz might be charming and, at times, manipulative, he is clearly not made in the image of Hannibal Lecter, nor of the FBI 'profilers' who stand against him and his kind. However much they added a veneer of complexity to the growing serial killer subgenre, *The Silence of the Lambs* and its kin remained in essence grimly intoxicating studies of evil. The moral world inhabited by Fitz, by contrast, is one painted less in black and white than in infinitely divisible shades of grey, owing less to modern Hollywood than to the traditions of understated British television realism, of *Z Cars* and *The Wednesday Play*.

Key to *Cracker*'s approach is Fitz's status as an outsider. By virtue of his professional experience and understanding of the criminal mind, he brings to investigations a very different approach from that of the police. While earlier British crime dramas, from *Juliet Bravo* (BBC, 1980–5) and *The Chinese Detective* (BBC, 1981–2) and on to *Prime Suspect*, had used outsiders within the force to explore its internal operation, and a series like *Public Eye* (ABC/Thames for ITV, 1965–75) employed a private investigator in a recognisable Chandler/Hammett tradition to present a more jaundiced view of the police, *Cracker* more properly belongs in a lineage of series offering a different perspective on police work by focusing on medical experts working alongside the police.

Filling a six-week gap between series of *Z Cars*, the now lost *Silent Evidence* (BBC, 1962) explored the cases of police pathologist Dr Martin Westlake (Basil Sydney). Contemporary *Radio Times* synopses and reviews suggest that one of the series' themes was the way in which forensic evidence served to undermine initial suppositions of the guilt of a key suspect. Similar ideas were something of a feature of the more successful *The Expert* (BBC, 1968–71; 1976). Its protagonist, Professor John Hardy (Marius Goring), a Home Office pathologist in a small Warwickshire town, was a slightly cantankerous hero, and one not inclined to hide his impatience with police impetuosity. Hardy's main police associate, DCI Fleming (Victor Winding), was a gruff, no-nonsense old-school detective, given to confident assumptions of guilt based on superficial evidence, and often irritated when Professor Hardy's detailed forensic work appeared to contradict his hunches. But Fleming was essentially fair-minded, and *The Expert*'s conclusions seemed more designed to encourage circumspection than to raise the alarm about miscarriages of justice. After the plot twists and turns necessary to sustain dramatic tension, Hardy frequently ended up providing the evidence to confirm, more or less, Fleming's initial hypothesis.

A more direct ancestor of Fitz is Herbert Lom's Harley Street psychiatrist Dr Corder, hero of the stylish 60s ITV drama *The Human Jungle*. Corder's cases were invariably psychosocial in origin, often highlighting dysfunctional family relationships, reflecting the then-fashionable theories of the 'anti-psychiatrist' R. D. Laing. When, as it occasionally did, his patients' behaviour brought them into contact with the law, Corder's concern for underlying causes and motivations represented a challenge to the more pragmatic concern with guilt and innocence of the police and criminal justice system. McGovern acknowledges *The Human Jungle*'s influence on *Cracker* by having Fitz compare Graham, therapist and rival for Judith's affections,

35

unfavourably with Herbert Lom ('To Say I Love You'), while elements of 'One Day a Lemming Will Fly' would seem to have been inspired – apparently unconsciously – by *The Human Jungle* episode 'Conscience on a Rack' (tx. 25/3/1965, in which a female schoolteacher, played by Flora Robson, recalls unfairly punishing a girl pupil to conceal a secret love for her). In 'To Be a Somebody', Fitz recounts to his own doctor his frustrations with the series: 'Well, you've told us what's wrong, Dr Corder, but that's all – where's the bloody cure?'

But if Fitz is unhappy with the way his fictional predecessor represented his profession, then his real-life counterparts had similar complaints about him. In preparing for the role, Coltrane had talked to the respected criminal profiler Dr Ian Stephen, who in 1969 had assisted in the ultimately unsuccessful police pursuit of Glasgow killer 'Bible John'. Stephen went on to serve as a consultant on *Cracker*, an experience he later described as 'interesting and positive' (Stephen, 1994). In the wake of the series' success, however, media references to forensic psychologists inevitably attracted the shorthand 'real-life Cracker', to the consternation of those in the field, who felt that Fitz was a poor advert for their work. Professor David Canter, arguably Britain's pre-eminent practitioner, complained to the *Daily Mail* (8 October 1994) that 'viewers must understand that Robbie Coltrane is not portraying a psychologist in any sense at all'.

It's common for professionals in any field to claim that television has misrepresented their work, but Canter has a point. McGovern freely acknowledges that he did little research in creating Fitz and, as we have seen, the character's approach has more in common with Catholic self-examination than psychology, a preference signalled by Fitz's disrespectful dismissal of the sacred cows of the discipline in his lecture in 'The Mad Woman in the Attic'. But *Cracker* ends up commenting on developments in the real world of forensic profiling in ways that its principal writer could never have anticipated.

As *Cracker*'s first series aired at the end of 1993, a case was unfolding which would bring the profession of forensic psychology more unwelcome attention than anything conceived by a television dramatist. It had begun in July 1992, with the murder of twenty-three-year-old Rachel Nickell, who was walking her dog on Wimbledon Common with her two-year-old son when she was attacked, sexually assaulted and stabbed forty-nine times. With few useful leads and under enormous public pressure, the police called in forensic psychologist Paul Britton, whose CV listed his involvement in a number of high-profile police investigations, among them the tragic murder of two-year-old James Bulger in Bootle, Liverpool.

The police investigation was focusing on Colin Stagg, a 'loner' with an interest in the occult who lived near Wimbledon Common, and whose background revealed a fantasy life of sexual dominance and sadism. With police encouragement, Britton devised an elaborate scheme in which an attractive, blonde, female detective, assuming the alias 'Lizzie James', began to exchange letters with Stagg expressing interest in fantasies similar to his own. A virgin with a history of rejections from women, Stagg was, as Britton hoped, entranced by the prospect of a sexual relationship that she tantalisingly held out. Over six months of letters, phone calls and meetings, 'Lizzie' encouraged his increasingly violent fantasies while slowly unveiling a fictitious past, concocted by Britton, in which she had, as a member of a Satanist coven, been involved in the ritual murder of a woman and child, insisting that 'I will only ever feel fulfilled again if I meet a man who has the same history as me' (Britton, 2001: 339). But despite her repeated entreaties, Stagg continued, apologetically, to deny the Nickell killing. Nevertheless, Britton was convinced. Stagg's fantasies, he told the police, revealed 'a highly deviant sexuality that's present in a very small number of men in the general population'. Despite the complete absence of forensic or any other evidence, the police decided to prosecute.

It was a costly own goal. Lord Justice Ognall ruled the evidence inadmissible, and in a strongly worded statement accused Britton and the police of 'a substantial attempt to incriminate a suspect by positive and deceptive conduct of the grossest kind'. Britton was likened to a 'puppet master', whose defence of his methods was 'highly disingenuous'. Nevertheless, Stagg was labelled 'the man who got away

37

with it,' by the tabloid press, encouraged by the police. Britton, meanwhile, continued to work as a profiler, publishing several successful books and frequently commenting in the media on criminal matters. In December 2008, Robert Napper, already in Broadmoor for a string of rapes and murders, confessed to and was convicted for killing Rachel Nickell. Britton had ruled out Napper as a suspect for the Wimbledon murder on the grounds that he failed to match his profile. Stagg finally won a full apology from the Metropolitan Police; Britton offered no such contrition.

Though he was then wholly unaware of the case (series one was already filmed by the time of the trial), in *Cracker*'s third story, 'One Day a Lemming Will Fly', McGovern created a scenario which shared strikingly similar characteristics: a high-profile, shocking crime, a plausible suspect without a convincing alibi, a public baying for justice, a police force desperate for a result and a forensic psychologist who allows his intuition of guilt to override his professional detachment. McGovern had already imagined for himself what would emerge as the lessons of the Britton/Stagg case – that police assumptions of guilt, based on flimsy evidence and supported by the professional opinion of an unchallenged 'expert', created a dangerous recipe for miscarriages of justice.

But in general, Fitz is, of course, a force for good. It is his intervention in 'The Mad Woman in the Attic' that prevents an earlier miscarriage of justice, and in later stories he frequently steers the police away from faulty assumptions. Nevertheless, his formidable intellectual gifts, coupled with the authority he accrues by virtue of his association with the police, make him a powerful figure, and at times he uses that power in ways that are selfish, manipulative or morally dubious.

It's interesting, in a series that has been accused, as Glen Creeber puts it, of 'reinstating the hard-drinking, hard-living male hero back at the centre of this traditionally masculine genre' (Creeber, 2002: 169), just how often Fitz's manipulative behaviour is couched in terms of his masculinity. In 'Mad Woman', in an attempt to persuade Penhaligon to pursue his hunch that the suspect, Kelly (Adrian Dunbar), is innocent, he traps her in a lift between floors, in a way that clearly parallels the male sexual threat to women explored throughout the series; later, he submits her to a cruel analysis of her sexual history, as a drastic last resort to help Kelly recover his lost memory. It is this sort of behaviour that leads Penhaligon (in 'To Be a Somebody') to describe Fitz as an 'emotional rapist'. In 'Brotherly Love', he embarks on a similarly intrusive interrogation of the sex life of Maggie Harvey (Bríd Brennan), wife of suspected prostitute killer David Harvey, causing her priest and brother-in-law, Father Michael (David Calder), to demand, 'Why doesn't he go the whole hog? Why doesn't he just rape her physically?'

This sense of Fitz's intellect as essentially predatory is one expression of the way in which elements of his character and behaviour mirror the criminals he pursues. In the typical crime narrative, a key feature of the successful detective is his ability to 'think like a criminal', just as *The Sweeney*'s Regan (John Thaw) and Carter (Dennis Waterman) inhabit a world of booze and womanising which parallels that of the armed robbers and gangsters they confront (see Clarke, 1986). Such 'villains', however violent and criminal, conformed to certain rules or codes and had readily comprehensible motives – chiefly, money. The killers and rapists of *Cracker*'s milieu, however, represent a greater imaginative challenge, one that demands Fitz's particular skill to explore the very darkest corners of his own psyche. 'Show me a man,' says Fitz in 'Men Should Weep', 'and I will show you a potential killer, a potential rapist. I *am* one, for goodness sake.' Only socialisation and fear, he argues, keep him and millions like him from acting on their worst instincts. It's a position barely divisible from that of the most radical feminists, suggesting that, however much he bristles at feminism ('Mad Woman' sees him baiting one of Judith's friends for the hypocrisy of paying subsistence wages to her cleaner while she teaches Women's Studies), he is prepared to accept much of its analysis.

In many ways Fitz is the epitome of 'unreconstructed' masculinity. He evades his responsibilities as a husband and father, seeking refuge in the traditional masculine pursuits of work, gambling and prodigious drinking (six or seven bottles of whisky a week, on top

39

of fifty to sixty cigarettes a day). He uses his intellect (and sometimes his physical size) to intimidate others into submission. Though he is, by virtue of his profession, highly emotionally articulate, he retreats into reticence and self-destructive behaviour when under stress. And, in his relationship with the much younger Jane Penhaligon (who he persistently belittles as 'Panhandle'),[4] he displays all the signs of a very traditional male 'mid-life crisis'.

'One Day a Lemming Will Fly', gives us a beautifully distilled demonstration of the cruel joy that Fitz can take in sexual manipulation. Still burning with the knowledge of Judith's adultery with Graham (David Haig), Fitz, already aware of Penhaligon's attraction to him, initiates a flirtatious conversation by popping a sweet in her mouth as they sit in her car:

> FITZ: It speaks volumes about a person, Panhandle, the way they suck a sherbet lemon. Me, I'm a cruncher. I like to pop 'em in, crunch, explosion of sherbet, instant gratification. Judith is a roller. She likes to roll 'em around her mouth for ages, noisily. You see, as a child, she got more pleasure out of making the other kids jealous than she did out of the sweetie itself. I think you're probably a sucker, am I right? I think you like to make it last.
> PENHALIGON: (*drawls suggestively*) Yeah.
> FITZ: I bet you could suck that sherbet lemon wafer thin before you got so much as a hint of sherbet.
> PENHALIGON: (*laughs, then sighs with satisfaction*) Yeah.
> FITZ: Thus indicating a massive guilt complex.

This analysis conforms to a pattern of Fitz's extemporised observations about the hidden meaning in apparently trivial unconscious behaviour (in the same line as Freud's analysis of everyday psychological phenomena – jokes, absent-mindedness, slips of the tongue – in *The Psychopathology of Everyday Life* (1901)). But the scene is also a fantastically controlled, and controlling, seduction. After the physically intimate act of placing the sweet in Penhaligon's mouth, Fitz cleverly insinuates Judith into the conversation, in such a way as to make her appear both belittled – rendered as a child – and undeserving of respect – because of her callous manipulation of her school friends. Meanwhile, he sustains a strong sexual undercurrent through his choice of words ('gratification', 'pleasure', 'suck'), which is picked up in the tone of Penhaligon's monosyllabic responses. The clear implication is that, where Judith is a manipulator, Penhaligon is somebody who can both deliver and enjoy gratification. But alongside this is the language of the 'con': Fitz identifies Penhaligon as a 'sucker', an easy target. Judith, meanwhile, is a 'roller': a player, a gambler, like Fitz himself. And having made his conquest, Fitz withdraws, skilfully displacing guilt onto his victim, presaging his similar retreat at the end of the story when, having accepted Penhaligon's rash invitation to join her on holiday, he leaves her waiting alone – like a 'sucker' – at the airport.

It may be an expression of Fitz's creator's own ambivalence about feminism that led to the casting of Barbara Flynn as Judith – the one piece of casting for which McGovern claims credit (McGovern, 2007a). Flynn gained a reputation for playing strong, intelligent, independent women, but before *Cracker* perhaps her best-known role was the sexually manipulative lesbian Dr Rose Marie in *A Very Peculiar Practice* (BBC, 1986–8), who rails against the 'phallocratic hierarchy' at Lowlands University, and makes withering, mock-pitying observations about the difficulties of being a man. Judith is an altogether less devious character, but she does stand as a forceful representative of womanhood, and the closest Fitz has to an intellectual equal.

Not that all of Fitz's victims are women. The most terrifying demonstration of his manipulative power casts him in the role of feminist avenger against his nemesis, Jimmy Beck, following the latter's rape of Penhaligon. In 'Brotherly Love', following Beck's repeated denials of Penhaligon's charge, Fitz takes it upon himself to force out the truth. Beck, just returned to work after a spell in a psychiatric hospital (ostensibly because of his grief and guilt over the murder of his boss, DCI Bilborough), is clearly in a highly vulnerable state. Cornering his quarry in a pub, Fitz begins with an ostensibly innocent enquiry into his health,

Fitz the tormentor

suggesting that he may be suffering the early symptoms of a heart attack. Having thus planted the seed of anxiety, he carefully and mercilessly nurtures it, breathlessly describing, and thereby feeding Beck's panic until the symptoms appear to become genuinely life-threatening:

> Your arteries are getting smaller and smaller and your heart's pumping and pumping. Your blood pressure is going up and up and up. You're head's swimming. You're going to die, Jimmy. You're going to die! Get it off your chest. Guilt suffocates. Get it off your chest! You have to tell me!

The ruse works, and Beck does confess, although Fitz is bound to secrecy by his own oath. But this is a Fitz claiming for himself the power of life and death: judge, jury and, very nearly, executioner. In our certainty of Beck's guilt (despite the absence, at this point, of any tangible proof), our horror at his crime and our sympathy for his victim, it's easy to lose sight of the fact that his confession is extracted by Fitz through the use of what is, in effect, torture.

If this is Fitz in his most fearsome aspect, a much earlier scene presents a no less manipulative Fitz to more comic effect. In 'To Say I Love You', Fitz reluctantly attends a meeting of Gamblers' Anonymous run by his therapist rival Graham. What follows is one of *Cracker*'s most cherishable scenes, as Fitz, like some diabolic tempter, urges the other members of the group not only to accept their addiction, but to embrace it, celebrate it. As the priggish Graham looks on helplessly, Fitz turns his session into an ersatz casino, producing a pack of playing cards and inviting his fellow addicts to bet on the turn of each card: 'How long's it been,' he challenges, 'since your hands were trembling and your heart was pounding and bowels turned to ice? How long since you were last alive?'

In the same scene, Fitz articulates the self-validating thrill of a win:

> Cocaine, heroin: they all cost you money. But to gamble and win – that
> buzz, that leap-and-punch-the-air buzz and 200 smackers on top – there's

43

Demonic tempter: Fitz subverts the Gamblers' Anonymous meeting

nothing like it on this Earth, eh? 'I was right. I've got a bit of paper in my hand that says I was right. I weighed up the odds, I studied the form, and I was right.'

McGovern has spoken openly about his own chronic gambling during the early years of his marriage, when he was capable of betting away a week's wages before returning home on a Friday (Day-Lewis, 1998). The writer drew upon his own addiction in his portrait of heroin abusers in his 1990 drama *Needle* (McGovern, 2007a), and gambling is Fitz's drug, just as Holmes turns to cocaine to stave off torpor:

'My mind', [Holmes] said, 'rebels at stagnation. Give me problems, give me work, give me the most abstruse cryptogram, or the most intricate analysis, and I am in my own proper atmosphere. I can dispense then with artificial stimulants. But I abhor the dull routine of existence. I crave for mental exaltation.' (Arthur Conan Doyle, *The Sign of Four*)

44

For Fitz, too, gambling offers exhilaration when ordinary life seems flat. His police work gives him a new sense of purpose and excitement, and when he is thrown back into the 'dull routine of existence', his gambling is at its most wanton. 'Life needs a bit of risk,' Fitz tells Judith. He rejects 'that long, straight, narrow, boring road' trod by the likes of Graham in favour of 'a bit of Bogart and Hepburn on the *African Queen*'. Though it never made it into the series, McGovern's character outline explains that Fitz's compulsion to take risks is behind his refusal to drive: 'it's just too tempting to put your foot down and close your eyes and gamble that you won't hit anything before you've counted to twenty' (Crace, 1995: 18). His compulsive risk-taking can make Fitz roguishly attractive – anti-establishment, devil-may-care – but it can be ugly too. Judith's first departure follows her discovery that, having already exhausted his bank overdraft and exceeded the limit on two credit cards, Fitz has forged her signature to fraudulently raise £5,000 on their mortgage. Judith has come to terms

Heroic gambler: apprehending Hennessy   45

with most of Fitz's faults, but his gambling is what drives her away
from him. 'Gambling hurts me, it hurts my children,' she insists in
'Brotherly Love'.

But Fitz's need for validation ('I was right'), for the satisfaction
of a bet won, is not just a character flaw; it is integral, too, to his success.
He studies his quarry as he studies horses' form in the *Racing Post*.
And he is never more impressive – or more alarming – than when he is
playing for the very highest stakes: hulking over the terrified Hennessy
(Nicholas Woodeson) on the railway track as a train looms in 'Mad
Woman'; goading the rapist Floyd while he has Judith at knifepoint in
'Men Should Weep'. Most astonishing is the climax of 'To Say I Love
You'. With a gas explosion imminent, Fitz, having already successfully
rescued the blind kidnap victim with only seconds to spare, delays his
own escape in favour of one more desperate effort to dissuade the
stammering Sean from self-sacrifice. Finally accepting the futility of his

task, he calmly walks away from the house, ignoring Penhaligon's anxious pleas for him to run. We can almost see him betting himself that he will reach safety before the blast. This, despite his earlier protestations ('I'm no hero, I know heroes – they're people who are too frightened to be cowards'), is his most heroic moment, and his most audacious defying of the odds.

Hand in hand with his risk-taking goes Fitz's gift for provocation. However much it wearies Judith, one of his most attractive qualities for us is the licence he has to say the things we daren't, whether it's telling a taxi driver, by way of a tip, 'lift your dahlias in the autumn', or winding up a pair of skinheads with a discourse on urinal etiquette. But such provocations, though entertaining for us, have their consequences. In detective fictions, the vulnerability of the hero is always an issue, but Fitz, perhaps because of McGovern's Catholic sense of justice, is particularly prone to putting himself in the way of punishment, from public humiliation (a faceful of wine for taunting Judith's feminist friend in 'The Mad Woman in the Attic'; a jug of iced water over his head for manipulating Penhaligon in 'To Say I Love You') to a severe beating and the theft of his winnings outside a casino in 'One Day a Lemming Will Fly', a bloody nose from the aforementioned skinheads in 'To Be a Somebody' and, in the same story, the indignity of a 'heart attack' that is revealed as nothing more than a panic attack. In 'Brotherly Love', he falls victim to a yuppie's weaponised mobile phone.

What's fascinating about this litany of punishments is the extent to which we are invited to enjoy them. While we might, for the most part, be awed by Fitz's gifts, we are far from blind to his deficiencies. And although he is, of course, *Cracker*'s most persistent focus, the narrative allows for other points of identification. The device of revealing most of the facts of almost every case early in the story allows us to recognise his genius, but it also shows us where his profile deviates from or misinterprets the truth. And in his arguments with Judith and Penhaligon, among others, Fitz is frequently and plainly in the wrong. At these moments, we see Fitz through others' eyes, and can examine the faults that he fails, despite his relentless self-examination, to recognise in himself.

Like all the best characters, Fitz is riddled with contradictions. He is a man of sharp insights who fails to foresee the consequences of his behaviour; who resents the rise of feminism but accepts its critique of masculinity; who is attracted to strong, intelligent women but can't help letting them down; who 'would die for' his family ('True Romance') but seems unable to maintain stable relationships with them. This is the shape of the man. But while he is clearly the most vivid character in *Cracker* – and one of the most vivid in all of 1990s television – the series, of course, is not *only* about Fitz. Still, it is Fitz who keeps us watching – amazed at his genius, entranced by his wit, sometimes appalled by his selfish or self-destructive behaviour, but never less than engrossed.

3 Understanding and Condemning

In February 1993, in the wake of the shocking murder of two-year-old James Bulger, Prime Minister John Major told the *Mail on Sunday* that as a society 'we should condemn a little more and understand a little less'. Major's declaration was later damned by Blake Morrison, author of a passionate analysis of the trial, *As If*, as 'one of the dimmest political slogans ever dreamed up' (Morrison, 2003), but it played well to his own restless constituency, and fitted the agenda of a press bent on retributive justice and scornful of politicians deemed 'soft on crime'.

That same February brought what became one of New Labour's most memorable soundbites, when Tony Blair, then shadow home secretary, promised that his party in government would be 'tough on crime, tough on the causes of crime'. It was a shrewd and resonant phrase, offering apparent reassurance to those in his own party who saw crime as fundamentally a problem of poverty, deprivation and inequality, while acknowledging that the victims of crime – the majority of them poor and disadvantaged themselves – deserved protecting. In practice, there was no paradigm leap; what Blair's words signalled was less a new 'Third Way' approach, combining prevention with firm but just punishment, than an invasive shift into traditional Conservative territory. Blair was determined to conquer the Tories' perceived natural advantage over Labour on law and order issues, even if it meant, in effect, aping their policies. Battle was joined in what would become an inflationary war of retribution.

While the political pendulum was swinging still further right on law and order, the safety of British justice was in question as never before, following the overturning of a succession of notorious wrongful convictions, many of them on the basis of falsely assumed IRA connections. The 1989 release of the Guildford Four, imprisoned for the 1974 Guildford pub bombing, was followed in 1991 by the Maguire Seven (minus Giuseppe Conlon, who died in prison in 1980) and the Birmingham Six; the following year mentally handicapped Stefan Kiszko, convicted in 1976 of murdering eleven-year-old Lesley Molseed, was released on appeal. Each prosecution had followed a particularly heinous crime, after which the police had responded to public and political pressure for swift justice with a catalogue of unlawful methods, from falsifying witness statements to obtaining confessions with beatings or other coercion and withholding evidence from the accused and their defence. This spate of quashed convictions renewed public anxieties about police accountability which, as Charlotte Brunsdon argues, can be traced in the crime drama of the early 1990s. Brunsdon cites particularly *Prime Suspect* and *Between the Lines* (BBC, 1992–5), highlighting their concern with 'two questions: "who can police?" and "who is accountable?" ' (Brunsdon, 1998: 226)

49

It's reasonable, as Brunsdon argues, to define *Cracker* as a 'transitional' work marking a point of generic change in the middle of the decade from the police procedural, which puts police detectives at the centre of the narrative, to a new focus on medical/scientific investigators (to an extent which places such characters, often quite artificially, at the forefront of investigations). But despite or even because of its non-police hero, *Cracker* is, it seems to me, no less concerned with interrogating modern policing than either *Prime Suspect* or *Between the Lines*, and rather more so than the medical/crime drama hybrids that follow it, from *Silent Witness* (BBC, 1996–) to *Waking the Dead* (BBC, 2001–). It comments directly on real cases: in 'To Be a Somebody', Fitz talks sarcastically of 'good old-fashioned British justice

– where a man's innocent until proven Irish', in a story that revolves around the Hillsborough disaster; in 'The Big Crunch', he compares the autistic Dean (Darren Tighe), wrongly suspected of the murder of Joanne Barnes (Samantha Morton), to Stefan Kiszko. It returns repeatedly, particularly during the first two series, to questions about the assumption of guilt and the risk of a false conviction. And finally, it explores issues around the internal operation of the force, especially in relation to the position of women.

The rise of non-police 'experts' in crime drama can be seen in part as a response to the issues raised by recent miscarriages of justice. The proliferation of such figures in the 'background' of TV crime dramas during the 1980s – and their move into the foreground with *Cracker* – reflects developments in the real world, but it also testifies to a concern that 'old-fashioned' detection methods are inadequate to cope not only with increasingly sophisticated criminals but with the need to restore public confidence in the security of convictions. In *Cracker*, Fitz is just one of an army of criminal psychologists (two others are consulted by the police in later episodes), pathologists, forensic scientists, 'scene-of-crime' experts, speech analysts, photographers and press officers who are seen as an essential element of the modern-day police force, and the extent to which the series' police characters accommodate or utilise their expertise – Fitz's in particular – becomes one way by which we can measure how far they are in step with the times.

The relationship between Fitz and his new police colleagues is from the outset coloured by antagonism. This has much to do with Fitz's combative personality and the inevitable conflict arising from his profession: psychology tends to be viewed with suspicion or even contempt by police officers who mistrust complex explanations of human behaviour. But more fundamental than this are Fitz's very different orientation to justice and his profound concern with motive.

When detectives – at least in fiction – talk of 'motive', they generally mean a *possible* reason to have committed the crime. Not, that is, necessarily the *actual* reason the crime was committed, but a logically satisfying explanation for the act, sufficient to begin mounting a convincing case of the suspect's guilt, or to pursue a particular line of inquiry. In other words, motive is *imputed*, not (or at least not necessarily) revealed or proven. The hypothesis may be useful to an investigation, but its confirmation is not essential in order for the case to be satisfactorily solved; more tangible evidence will eventually supersede it. In the course of an investigation, several suspects with an apparent motive may be eliminated, but even after a conviction has been attained, the *real* motive may never be revealed.

Fitz's understanding of motive is very different, as we have seen. Although, in Holmes fashion, he proves himself adept at spotting clues that the police miss (the fragments of hair on the alley wall in 'To Say I Love You', the significance of the small change on the newsagent's floor in 'To Be a Somebody'), he looks inward for a deeper understanding of the criminal, making an imaginative journey into his or her psyche. This approach elicits scepticism among the ranks of 'no-nonsense', 'common sense'-oriented police. But it is Fitz's challenge to the police's instinct-driven approach to guilt that represents the greatest affront to his antagonists in the force. The 'good cop' feels guilt or innocence 'in his guts'. The need for evidence or a confession is a burden to the instinct-driven policeman, an obstacle to the summary justice he considers himself equipped to deliver (Westlake, 1980). But instinct in detective work is a faith position. In *Cracker*, instinct leads to assumptions and, potentially, to miscarriages of justice or even deaths.

Fitz's most vociferous opponent in the Greater Manchester Police Force is Detective Sergeant Jimmy Beck. Beck is an archetypal 'instinct-driven' copper, a reactionary, 'hang 'em and flog 'em' refugee from a mythical bygone age of policing in which a 'clip round the ear' is a deterrent against juvenile delinquency; intimidation and brutality constitute effective law enforcement; and justice is of the Old Testament variety. He thrives on the confrontation of police work and on the licence it gives him to exert his physical authority; there is no room in his black-and-white world for 'softly, softly' approaches to crime based on rehabilitation or prevention: 'I want 20 serious crimes a day – I enjoy

51

them. They pass the time. Ovies [overtime] as well. Bollocks to prevention' ('To Say I Love You').

Beck is characteristic of a species of policeman already familiar on British screens by the early 90s, and one that demonstrates changes in television's and society's attitudes to policing since the 1970s, when the violence and routine rule-breaking of *The Sweeney*'s DI Jack Regan and DS George Carter were seen as a necessary response to the increasing brutality of the criminal underworld. By the end of the 1970s, however, the perils of this 'by any means necessary' approach to fighting crime were already coming under scrutiny. G. F. Newman's *Law and Order* (BBC, 1978) presented a Special Branch habitually accepting cash incentives from the criminal fraternity to 'look the other way', while enforcing the law on the principle of 'muggins' turn'. A decade later, *The Bill*, which in its earliest days had presented a more or less uncritical view of London policing, was enticing viewers with the spectacle of an unadulterated 'hard man' copper of the old school. DI Burnside (Christopher Ellison) was a brutal, rule-breaking thief-taker of the Jack Regan type, but one whose methods, however effective, were frequently presented as a liability to his colleagues and the force. Such 'hard men' were now seen as dangerously out of step with the demands of modern policing and the necessity for the force to be seen to be fair, honest and accountable.

These concerns were the meat of *Between the Lines*, created by former *Bill* writer J. C. Wilsher. The series focused on the cases of Detective Superintendent Tony Clark (Neil Pearson) of the Complaints Investigation Bureau, an internal police department set up to investigate and, if necessary, prosecute charges of corruption and wrongdoing within the force. *Between the Lines* explored issues ranging from corruption to brutality, 'fit-ups', deaths in custody, racism and sexism within the force. The episode 'The Only Good Copper' (tx. 23/10/1992) deals with an investigation into the death of an officer who is killed on duty as a result of the failure of his colleagues to come to his aid in time. It emerges that the dead officer had a history of brutal overreaction to trouble and that he was considered a risk to the safety and reputation of his colleagues, who, without ever intending his death, collectively decided to teach him a lesson by withholding assistance. One of those colleagues, PC Bilton, justifies his actions by telling Clark, 'We can't afford the hard men, sir, not any more. . . . the cost is too high. He'd become a liability.' PC Bilton, interestingly, is played by Colin Tierney, subsequently Beck's colleague DC Harriman in the second series of *Cracker*.

Fitz's analytical, empathetic approach represents for Beck a soft, 'feminine' challenge to his own rigidly masculine absolutism. He might be seen as a one-man 'crisis of masculinity'. This term gained currency in the late 1980s and 1990s to describe the state of siege in which men perceived themselves in a culture in which not only were traditional masculine roles held up to stern criticism by feminism, but where the labour roles that had sustained male identity in the industrial age were increasingly swept aside by high unemployment and the radical reorientation of industry (from manufacturing to services) of the Thatcher and Reagan era. Unable to march in step with this changing world, Beck is left clinging to his old moral certainties as he feels himself engulfed in a tide of feminisation, of which Fitz, in his way, is a part: 'Compassion – the job's full of it. Full of women, full of rape counsellors, full of victim support counsellors,' he complains in 'Brotherly Love'.

By comparison, Beck's superior, DCI Bilborough, seems in many ways a model policeman. He is young, dynamic, attractive, apparently a perfect blend of the most desirable characteristics of 'old-school' male police officer and the sensitivities demanded of new masculinity. He is a concerned husband, who takes time out of his schedule to worry about his wife's pregnancy ('One Day a Lemming Will Fly') and attends the birth of their child ('To Be a Somebody'). He shows alarm at Beck's excesses ('Don't know about him, but you terrified me,' he exclaims, after witnessing his subordinate's aggressive questioning of the suspect in 'The Mad Woman in the Attic'), and is sufficiently forward-thinking to call upon Fitz's help, overriding Beck's reservations. But Christopher Eccleston's charismatic performance shouldn't blind us to Bilborough's manifest flaws.

53

Faces of the
modern police
force:
DCI Bilborough
(Christopher
Eccleston)

DS Beck
(Lorcan
Cranitch)

DS Penhaligon
(Geraldine
Somerville)

References to Bilborough's youth and inexperience pepper *Cracker*'s early stories, and his encounters with more experienced professionals repeatedly point up his own deficiencies. In 'To Say I Love You' he is criticised by a senior fireman for neglecting to find out vital information about a house under siege. In 'One Day a Lemming Will Fly' he irritates a senior pathologist when he pulls him from a fancy dress party (in one of McGovern's more elaborately comic scenes) to confirm that the death of young Timothy Lang (Wesley Cook) was murder, not suicide – a conclusion that ought to be obvious – then is rebuked by his boss for his mishandling of a disorderly public demonstration in which he ends up arresting Tim's father (Tim Healy) and brother, Andy (Lee Philip Hartney). Such incidents raise questions about Bilborough's judgment. But the chief standard by which the series measures him and his police colleagues is their concern for justice. On this measure, Bilborough, like Beck, falls far short of expectations.

Cracker foregrounds its concerns with injustice in the two stories that open and close the first series. The first, 'The Mad Woman in the Attic', shows a miscarriage of justice narrowly averted, the other, 'One Day a Lemming Will Fly', sees an innocent man sent to prison for the sake of avoiding police embarrassment. The two stories stand apart in preserving the 'whodunnit' structure of the conventional detective narrative; in almost every other *Cracker* story, the perpetrators are identified more or less from the start.[5] This departure from the series' usual *modus operandi* is necessary because the central concern of both stories is the assumption of guilt based on incomplete evidence.

'Mad Woman' proceeds from an almost perfectly Hitchcockian premise[6] – a young woman is butchered on a train, the latest in a series of brutal, bloody murders; a man (Adrian Dunbar) is discovered unconscious by the railway tracks, his clothes stained with blood. Police assume his guilt, but he claims complete amnesia. This last aspect provides the justification for Bilborough's enlisting of Fitz, who has a personal interest, given that the victim was his student. But while Fitz initially shares Bilborough's scepticism at the suspect's convenient memory loss, he soon begins to doubt his guilt (proceeding from a classic Holmesian observation: the suspect, soon identified as Francis Kelly, doesn't wear a watch, but the killer is a regular train-user – 'people who use trains wear a watch'). By now, however, Bilborough's certainty is impervious to argument, especially when it comes with a side order of Fitz's self-righteousness: 'You've got yourself a suspect, so all your energy's concentrated into proving that he did it. You could prove he didn't do it, but where would that get you? Classic policing error.'

Fitz's continuing disagreement with Bilborough ultimately gets him thrown off the case, but he does eventually, in partnership with the more open-minded DS Jane Penhaligon, prove Kelly's innocence and catch the real killer, winning for himself and Penhaligon a grudging respect. But Fitz is himself guilty of an equivalent 'classic policing error' in 'Lemming'. The suspect here is a teacher and the victim his pupil, fourteen-year-old Timothy Lang, who has been found hanging in woodland – an even more emotive crime than the butchering of women in 'Mad Woman', which, in its furious public reaction (if not in its details) recalls the murder of James Bulger in McGovern's Liverpool in the previous year.

As is common in child murders, initial suspicion falls on the immediate family – mother, father, and elder brother, Andy – but attention soon turns to the boy's English teacher, Cassidy (Christopher Fulford), after a threat of suicide (which ends with Fitz persuading him not to jump from the roof of a shopping centre) offers apparent evidence of a guilty conscience. We first encounter Cassidy in boxing gloves, pummelling a punching bag in the gym when Fitz and Penhaligon visit his school. 'It saves me doing it to the kids', he jokes, adding: 'The art of teaching today – just keeping your hands off the little bastards.' In the charged context of the murder of one of his pupils, this offhand remark takes on a darkly sexual tone: 'doing it', of course, is schoolboy slang for sex, while the idea that Cassidy has to work to keep his 'hands off' his young charges suggests both repressed sexual urges and an awareness of

Exaggerated masculine display: Cassidy   57

a latent capacity for violence that needs to find a safe release. Fitz's own
suspicions are raised when, in answer to his question 'Do you live
alone?', Cassidy announces, 'I'm thinking of getting married.'
This unnecessary volunteering of information reinforces the sense of
exaggerated masculine display.

The case against Cassidy thereafter proceeds directly from the
assumption of his homosexuality. By the time Fitz has 'rescued' him
from the rooftop, he is convinced that the teacher is gay – or rather, as he
puts it to Cassidy, '*you* think you're gay'. Beck arrives just in time to
hear this exchange, and it is he who alerts the angry crowd outside the
station that the police have 'picked up a shirtlifter'. From this moment
on, Cassidy *becomes* gay – whether the label reflects his true sexuality is
as academic for Fitz as it is for the police and the restless mob, in whom
this revelation awakens old mythical associations of homosexuality and
paedophilia.

The febrile atmosphere surrounding the case, including a near riot outside the police station when Cassidy is brought in, contributes to a sense of a man under siege, literally so when Tim's father attacks his home with a mechanical digger. But so, too, does Fitz, who takes it upon himself to announce Cassidy's homosexuality to his girlfriend, helping to bring about the end of their relationship. It is Fitz who spells out for Cassidy his bleak choices: 'Confess, plead guilty – it'll be over in a flash. Deny it – there'll be a trial; week upon week, detail upon detail, your mother squirming and cringing.' Eventually, after a long three-sided battle on the terrain of masculinity and homophobia between Fitz, Beck and Cassidy, Fitz extracts from Cassidy his confession with a promise to 'share your burden', setting up the story's shock conclusion. For despite his confession, and the certainty of Fitz and his police colleagues, Cassidy is not Tim's killer, as he ultimately reveals from his cell, revelling in Fitz's discomfort as the psychologist digests his error: 'What's wrong, Fitz? An innocent man's confessed? The killer's still out there? No – you were wrong! That's what's bothering you, isn't it?'

58 McGovern himself was not pleased with 'Lemming'. It was written in a hurry, after the original script by another writer was rejected. To fully accept the conclusion, as he concedes, we have to believe that Cassidy could be so tortured by guilt for his role in Tim's death (it was his rejection of the boy, the teacher believes, that sent him into the path of his killer) that he is willing to submit himself to a prison term and the unenviable status of a 'nonce' by way of atonement (McGovern, 2007a). Nevertheless, perhaps its short deadline is what gives 'Lemming' its urgency, for it is one of the series' most frenzied stories, bubbling with concentrated rage and sharply insightful about the pressures that undermine justice. It is a bold writer, too, who dares so completely to undermine his hero.

For this is *Cracker*'s most profoundly desolate conclusion. We have become accustomed to Fitz's feet of clay in his personal life, but until now we have been reassured that as a detective, at least, he is a man of rare insights and integrity. Cassidy's charge – 'you were wrong!' – cuts to the core of Fitz's self-belief, inverting his gambler's cry of validation

Cassidy's pointing
finger

'You were wrong!'

59

('I was right!'). His once awe-inspiring ability to sniff out guilt is
revealed as a crude tool, inadequate to distinguish between real
culpability and the feelings of self-blame that frequently accompany
violent death. Fitz is guilty of an error as grave as Bilborough's in 'Mad
Woman' – working backwards from the presumption of guilt to the
satisfyingly plausible motive. It's rare enough that crime fiction denies us
the satisfaction of a just resolution (despite the filing cabinets stuffed
with unsolved cases that surely litter all police stations). But here we are
presented with a grotesque injustice in which our hero is unmistakably
implicated. 'It's the *truth* that counts, not the *result*,' Fitz insists in a
desperate, but ultimately unsuccessful bid to persuade Bilborough to
reverse his mistake and cancel the scheduled press conference. For the

policeman, such a retreat is too awful to contemplate. 'You want me to tell the boss I was wrong?', he demands, 'I'd be back pounding the bloody beat. You want me to tell that lot out there I was wrong? They'd lynch me. You want me to tell his mother I was wrong?'

The truth versus the result: this opposition is *Cracker*'s own – real justice and the demands of the criminal justice system are, in such a charged scenario, perversely incompatible. The story devastatingly shows how the hysteria surrounding a particularly notorious crime creates a demand for swift action that overwhelms the slow and steady process of true justice. An angry and distraught family; a vengeful, frightened public, urged on by a baying media; an ambitious investigating officer; a police leadership desperate for a result – all these conspire to make a perversion of justice not just possible, but dangerously probable.

But if this is a radical conclusion, especially for a mainstream TV crime drama, it is one from which *Cracker* ultimately withdraws, as it probably must if the series is to continue. By the beginning of the next story, 'To Be a Somebody', Fitz has apparently made good on his threat to cut all ties with Bilborough and the Manchester police. But he is soon back, and trying once again to push blame onto Bilborough, who defiantly insists, 'I did my job'. Fitz's retort is nothing if not robust – 'Suddenly I smell gas ovens and six million burning corpses' – but the moment passes. After Bilborough's death in the same story, his replacement, DCI Wise (Ricky Tomlinson), inspects Fitz's records and remarks, 'you get results'. It's a word, by now, pregnant with meaning, and we might remember that the list of 'results' Wise is reading must conclude with the travesty of the Cassidy conviction. But with Bilborough is also buried Fitz's most profound mistake; Bilborough's memory lingers, but Cassidy is soon forgotten.

If much of *Cracker* offers us a bleak vision of the police, it does at least present us with one more appealing representative of the force in the form of DS Penhaligon. Sensitive, empathetic and thoughtful, she embodies a set of 'female' characteristics wholly different from the aggressively masculine traits exhibited by Bilborough and Beck.

But Penhaligon's is a story of undervalued ability and potential that was, by the early 1990s, revealed as alarmingly common for women serving in the police force.

The denial of opportunities to women in the force was highlighted in 1992 with the case of Alison Halford. Halford had risen through the ranks to become Britain's most senior woman police officer as Deputy Chief Constable in the Merseyside Police Force, but once there she found her career stalled and watched as more junior, less able colleagues overtook her in the police hierarchy, while her own applications for promotion were repeatedly blocked or rejected. Exasperated, she eventually turned to the Equal Opportunities Commission for help, at which point her senior colleagues and their allies in the local Police Authority began a sustained campaign to undermine her (Halford, 1993).

Halford's experience put on public display the lengths to which the all-male police elite was prepared to go to protect its privileges, and the reverberations of the case can be felt in several crime dramas of the early 1990s, most obviously *Prime Suspect*, where Halford's account added credence to Jane Tennison's own experiences at the hands of unsympathetic male superiors. In the second series of *Between the Lines*, the female member of the team, DS Maureen ('Mo') Connell (Siobhan Redmond), becomes increasingly radicalised, partly through her contact with a senior female officer, played by Dearbhla Molloy and clearly modelled on Halford, who is the victim of a malicious disciplinary case launched by her senior colleagues. Mo eventually takes the bold step of coming out as a lesbian (a charge repeatedly levelled at Halford).

Like Mo, *Cracker*'s Penhaligon (she is hardly ever called 'Jane') is more junior than Halford, and hasn't yet hit her head on the promotional 'glass ceiling' (indeed, both ultimately reach the next rank of inspector).[7] But Mo is at least treated with respect by her team and plays a role commensurate with her rank and ability. Penhaligon, by contrast, is assigned tasks apparently tailored to her 'feminine' traits, from dealing with grieving relatives and counselling rape victims to making tea, while the meat of the investigations is handled by

61

Bilborough and Beck. It is precisely the promise of a more active role held out by Fitz that entices her to accept his offer of partnership.

Both Mo and Penhaligon have evidently managed to make some progress in the force by playing 'one of the lads', participating in the hard-drinking culture and accepting or enduring the sexual humour and slurs of their male colleagues. Long before she 'comes out', Mo is the subject of malevolent whispers that she is a 'dyke'; Penhaligon has to put up with her boss's intrusive jokes about her sex life ('One Day a Lemming Will Fly') and with 'playful' simulated sex with, consecutively, her colleague DC Giggs (Ian Mercer) and Fitz during a reconstruction of the alleyway passion of murderous young lovers Sean and Tina (Susan Lynch) ('To Say I Love You').

In 'Men Should Weep', during an otherwise all-male drinking session which interrupts the investigation into the masked serial rapist Floyd, Penhaligon gamely laughs along with DCI Wise's story about an eighty-year-old woman reporting a rape that occurred sixty-one years earlier ('I don't want to charge anyone,' goes the punchline, 'I just wanna talk about it'), but she takes issue with Beck's declaration that women 'allow themselves to be raped' because 'subconsciously they want it'. Her opposition to Beck's argument wins her the support of both Fitz and Wise, and Beck's aggressive demands as to whether she has ever had rape fantasies earn him a (mild) rebuke from the DCI. During the same exchange, however, DC Harriman's comment about wanting to give (Tory government minister) Virginia Bottomley 'a bloody good spanking' wins Wise's approving response, 'you're twisted, and you're a pervert, and you'll make a bloody good policeman'. Similarly, Wise's sympathy for Penhaligon has its limits. He dismisses her question about Beck's suitability to police a rape case. 'You'd go off the case before Beck, love,' he tells her, before instructing her to 'forget the feminists and the hairy-arsed lesbians [and] go back and have a drink with your mates'. Penhaligon may be accepted, to an extent, as 'one of the lads', but her challenge to masculine discourse is interpreted not only as overreaction, but as evidence of extremism and sexual aberration.

But while Beck's comments in the bar may represent only a minor transgression for his male colleagues, they are merely the first stage in a journey that will end with him irrevocably crossing the line between police and criminal. Shortly afterwards, Penhaligon organises a reconstruction of the rape of one of Floyd's victims (Floyd himself walks unnoticed among the bystanders). As the young woman retraces her steps in a suburban park, Beck, masked and clothed in the garb of the rapist, leaps out from behind a building. Her terrified response clearly has a profound effect on Beck, which we take to be a belated recognition of the horror of rape. In the light of later events, however, the reconstruction takes on a new meaning, as a *dress rehearsal* for Beck's rape of Penhaligon, the plot arc that runs through Jimmy McGovern's last two *Cracker* stories and gives actors Geraldine Somerville and Lorcan Cranitch the chance to take the spotlight.

Penhaligon's rape allows her, and us, to examine modern police responses to rape over a decade after the force was obliged to re-evaluate its procedures in the wake of Roger Graef's explosive fly-on-the-wall documentary *Police* (BBC, 1982), which showed an aggressive interrogation of a woman reporting rape and led to a public outcry. Despite her experience as a rape counsellor, only by going through the process herself does Penhaligon come to understand (and to demonstrate) the temptation to wash away the evidence of rape, to leave it unreported and avoid the trauma of invasive medical tests and emotionally draining questions from insensitive, sceptical or disbelieving investigators.

Changes in police procedures in the 1980s did lead to an increase in the reporting of rape, but proportionately fewer cases actually resulted in conviction. Of 1985's 1,842 recorded rapes, 450 (24 per cent) led to a conviction. In 1994, the year Penhaligon had her firsthand experience of the system, there were 5,039 recorded rapes but only 460 convictions (9 per cent).[8] Worse, contemporary studies suggest that sexual harassment remained alarmingly prevalent within the police force, and that reporting rape or abuse tended to rebound on the victim, as colleagues and senior officers looked upon complaints as a breach of

64   Awkward sympathy: Tom Carter attempts to comfort his raped wife,
Catherine

loyalty (Gregory and Lees, 1999). Though he professes (qualified) support, Wise sets out a similar argument after Penhaligon accuses Beck: 'You're making wild allegations against a bloody good officer. That's what they're going to think . . . . They're gonna be out there on their own with you. You might decide to scream rape again.'

Central to *Cracker*'s rape storyline are the flailing attempts of men to find an appropriate response. Particular attention is paid to Tom Carter (John McArdle), husband of rape victim Catherine (Marian McLoughlin), whose struggle to find a way to come to terms with his wife's ordeal leads him to vent his anger on an innocent suspect. Penhaligon's well-meaning colleagues, meanwhile, are clumsy in their expressions of sympathy after her rape. On her return to work, she is greeted in turn by Fitz, DC Harriman and PC Skelton (Wilbert Johnson), each offering sympathy or support but each crassly, if unwittingly, behaving in a way that revives memories of her ordeal: Fitz lies in wait for her in the car park (much as her assailant did elsewhere), while Skelton steps suddenly from a side room as she walks down the corridor and Harriman runs at her from behind to deliver his message.

The rape tests all of Penhaligon's colleagues, but it is most of all a challenge for Fitz. He doesn't start well, missing the significance of her burning her sullied clothes and making a crass joke about feminism ('I'm greatly in favour of women's movements: I hate it when they just lie there'). It is Fitz, however, acting as therapist rather than lover, who helps Penhaligon to marshal the facts – her assailant's leather gloves, his whisky and tobacco breath, his aftershave – she needs to begin her investigation. But Fitz's support is undermined by the surprise return of a heavily pregnant Judith after several months' absence; the impending arrival of his third child demands from him a renewed commitment to his family at the precise moment when Penhaligon most needs his help, forcing her to carry out her investigation alone. As the pursuit of Floyd literally leads Fitz back to Judith (who is now Floyd's quarry, following his pattern of targeting the wives and girlfriends of his enemies), the narrative focus divides, with Penhaligon's independent investigation into Jimmy Beck splitting off from the 'official' one (just as she and Fitz embarked on their illicit pursuit of Hennessy in 'Mad Woman'). This symbolic splitting of their partnership – both professional and sexual – is prefigured by an earlier scene in which she cuts short Fitz's attempt to discuss Judith's return. 'I have been *raped*,' she reminds him, 'Everything else pales into insignificance. Even you.'

65

Interestingly, the revelation of Beck's guilt is achieved not by means of 'masculine' deduction, but by a combination of 'feminine' qualities. When she encounters a Beck visibly upset following his visit to Bilborough's widow, Penhaligon moves to comfort him. This gesture of empathy brings her close enough to smell his aftershave, and to recognise it as the one worn by her attacker. Just as in the first *Prime Suspect*, where a female officer's spotting of the common link between the victims – nail extensions – provides a vital clue linking them to the suspect via his wife (a manicurist), an observation that emerges from

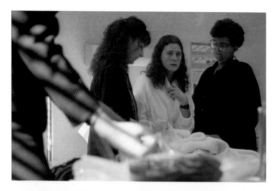

Penhaligon:
from victim . . .

to avenger

female terms of reference (a familiarity with beauty treatments, the
ability to distinguish different scents), points to a solution of the enigma
where conventional 'male' detection methods have either stalled or been
obstructed (Brunsdon, 1998).

But the conclusion of her pursuit of Beck sees Penhaligon
throw off any residue of passive victimhood in favour of an approach
that explicitly mimics male sexual aggression and returns the kind of
'low-level' harassment she has earlier endured. Having broken into his
apartment, she surprises the returning Beck with his own gun, forcing
him onto the floor then sitting astride him and inserting the barrel into
his mouth and demanding that he 'suck it', adding, as he protests, 'don't
speak with your mouth full' – a recitation of one of Bilborough's sexual

jokes in 'Lemming'. It is a sexual role reversal that recalls the rape revenge scenario of *Thelma and Louise* (1991), which had a huge cultural impact on its release for its celebration of female emancipation from abusive masculinity via the barrel of a gun. Penhaligon's act of self-determination seems to have been similarly satisfying for female viewers, and the cliffhanger ending of 'Men Should Weep', which leaves us wondering whether or not she has pulled the trigger, was certainly effective in retaining audience interest – the first episode of the next story, 'Brotherly Love', attracted the series' biggest audience to date. But Beck's death at Penhaligon's hand would suit neither *Cracker*'s moral agenda – there is no nobility in revenge – nor the character: as she tells Fitz in 'Brotherly Love', it wasn't the 'guts' to pull the trigger that she lacked, but the 'callousness'. Instead, Beck delivers his own justice by jumping from the roof of Manchester's towering Ramada Hotel, confirming Fitz's earlier intimation of the power of guilt.

The marginalisation, harassment and abuse recounted by Alison Halford and others and dramatised in the characters of Jane Penhaligon, Mo Connell and Jane Tennison amount to a charge of what might, slightly anachronistically, be termed 'institutional sexism' in the police force of the early 1990s – in line with the conclusions of the 1999 MacPherson Report into the handling of the murder of black teenager Stephen Lawrence that the Metropolitan Police Force was 'institutionally racist'. Interestingly, *Cracker* seems relatively unconcerned with racism within the force, nor does it portray the kind of embedded corruption explored by *Law and Order* or *Between the Lines*, both of which take their tone from the revelations about real-life police corruption that emerged during the 1970s and 80s. *Cracker*'s coppers aren't on the make, or even particularly dishonest, but they are prone to the kind of negligence, inhumanity and disregard for justice that led to the horrific tragedy and injustice of Hillsborough. In their different ways, most of McGovern's early stories for *Cracker* reflect the writer's abiding rage at Hillsborough and its symbolic representation of the progressive abandonment of the white working class. But the tragedy is represented in its most concentrated form in the story that began the second series,

67

Spokesman for working-class alienation: Albie

and which is, for most viewers, the series' most resonant and memorable story, and certainly its most personal.

Through the vengeful Hillsborough survivor Albie, who, in the wake of his father's death, shaves his head and exorcises his anger and bitterness in a series of brutal murders, McGovern vicariously enacts his own revenge for Hillsborough, killing both a policeman and a *Sun* reporter. In a sign of ambivalence towards his creation, he even kills a forensic psychologist. From Albie's mouth comes, unleavened, McGovern's bitter analysis of the demonisation and betrayal of the white working class, while Albie's abandonment of his moral and political values as a committed socialist, trade unionist and lifelong Labour supporter mirrors McGovern's own rejection of ideology.

Albie is an articulate spokesman for working-class anger and alienation. An intelligent, cultured man, he reads the *Guardian*, knows how to spell Rottweiler, and can identify Mozart's *Piano Concerto in C*

Major. He is employed – as a skilled labourer (a welder) – and a father, divorced but conscientious in supporting his wife and daughter. He is also a Liverpool football supporter, who attended, with his father, the FA cup semi-final on 15 April 1989. And he has been a devoted son, nursing his father through a slow, painful death. Cancer killed his father but, for Albie, 'It started at Hillsborough.'

'Treat people like scum, they start acting like scum.' So Albie justifies his metamorphosis, and his adoption of the uniform of a skinhead, the emblem of working-class thuggery, testifies to his transformation into an outrider for a grim future – a working class pushed beyond its limits and rising up, not in revolution, but in wild, uncontrollable violence. 'You're looking at the future,' Albie tells Fitz, 'this country's gonna blow, and people like me are gonna light the fuse: the despised, the betrayed.' Fitz, meanwhile, summons up from the pit of his depression his own more poetic but equally ugly prophecy:

> Post-nuclear war; all life obliterated. There's a mattress in a pool at the bottom of a block of flats. Storm after storm, the water lifts up the mattress, drops it, lifts it up, drops it, lifts it up, drops it – until finally, one day, the mattress crawls out of the pool. That's the start of a new evolutionary cycle – a sodden, stinking mattress.

The two visions are in essence the same – the supplanting of society by its unloved detritus. McGovern's own forecast at the time was similarly bleak: 'The vacuum on the Left is going to be filled by fascism,' he predicted, 'Within 15 years this country is going to have a fascist government' (McGovern, 1995).

We get a taste of this terrifying vision when Bilborough and his officers raid a skinhead club. The hall is decked with swastikas, racist propaganda, images of Hitler and the Klan. The sweating, writhing mass of bodies suggests some nightmare of regressed humanity, an orgy of idiot malevolence in DM boots. It's a future that evokes Orwell's *Nineteen Eighty-Four*, with its gruesome image of 'a boot stamping on a human face – for ever'. In other respects, McGovern's grim dystopia

Prophecy of a grim future: the skinhead club

recalls the arbitrary injustices of Terry Gilliam's fantastical *Nineteen Eighty-Four* update, *Brazil* (1985), with which 'To Be a Somebody', despite its naturalist aesthetic, shares some narrative elements.[9]

'People need to believe. People need to congregate,' says Albie, 'But there's nothing left to believe in, nothing left to congregate for. Only football.' For McGovern, the popular image today of the working class is inextricably tied up with football, the sole surviving mass working-class pursuit in an era that has seen all other vestiges of working-class pride, from the traditional industries of coalmining, textiles and engineering to the historic links between organised labour and the political party that bore its name, swept away. When the behaviour of a minority of troublemakers became an excuse for the contemptuous and aggressive treatment of *all* football supporters, the tragedy of Hillsborough was, for Albie as for McGovern, inevitable. Hillsborough marks the culmination of the attack on white working-class culture that began on the right and was joined from the left, and in the wake of the disaster, everything Albie once believed lies in crumbles, leaving nothing but hatred and fury:

> We go to the match. They march us along. They slam us against walls, they treat us like scum. We look for help. We're socialists, we're trade unionists, and we look to the Labour Party for help. But we're not queers, we're not black, we're not Paki. There's no brownie points in speaking out for us, so the Labour Party turns its back. And we're not getting treated like scum any more. We're getting treated like wild animals. And yeah, one or two of us start acting like wild animals, and the cages go up and ninety-six people die.

Albie's shaven head is, on one level, a homage to his dead father, bald from chemotheraphy – he even begins by shaving a grave-shaped patch on his crown. But the act also calls to mind both the alienated, defiant skinhead Trevor in Alan Clarke's *Made in Britain* and the similarly disaffected Travis Bickle, who gives himself a Mohawk cut in Martin Scorsese's *Taxi Driver* (1975) – like Bickle, Albie is 'a man who would not take it any more'. But a more immediate parallel appears in Joel Schumacher's alarming, if politically ambivalent, *Falling Down* (1992), in which Michael Douglas's 'D-Fens' (not a skinhead, but with a military-style 'buzz-cut') takes arms against a sea of frustrations from the petty (a fast-food restaurant refusing to serve breakfast at 11 am) to the genuine (a heavily armed Latino gang). Like Albie, he begins his orgy of violence with an attack on an Asian (Korean) shopkeeper in protest at his prices.

To Albie, the shopkeeper Ali is a 'robbing Paki bastard' in a country 'full of robbing bastards'; to Ali, as his bereaved daughter later tells Fitz, 'white people are thieves'. Both are victims of poverty. The boarded-up shops neighbouring his indicate that Ali has had to struggle to survive in hard times; Albie has his own struggle, working nights to pay maintenance to his wife and daughter. And poverty, however unjust, still engenders shame. When he is four pence short for his *Guardian* newspaper and teabags, Albie senses he has lost face, and

71

Graven image:
Albie's homage

when his attempt at compromise is refused, he has only two options: confrontation or humiliating retreat. Each man, for reasons stemming from his own hardship, sticks rigidly to his position on a point of principle – so rigidly that one will die for it. Ali's death is a symptom of a tragic truth: poverty and prejudice divide those who should unite in battle against their causes. Meanwhile, in more comfortable surroundings, Fitz is showering an unmoved Judith with his casino winnings.

On the bus after the killing, Albie, distraught, comforts himself – as he will repeatedly when his conscience is troubled – with football chants. By the time he gets home, however, he has already begun to rationalise his action. To convince himself that the murder has meaning, that it isn't, in Fitz's words, 'just another stupid racist killing', more must die – one for each victim of Hillsborough. Ali's purposeless death, an action born of a petty slight and unendurable grief, becomes, in retrospect, an act of righteous vengeance for a catalogue of injustices against the white working class. In reality, the symbolic relevance to Hillsborough of most of his victims is highly dubious. Albie's second victim, the forensic psychologist professor Nolan, is arguably guilty of a simplistic class stereotype (his unimaginative 'profile' concludes that Ali's killer is an unemployed fascist), but what appears to upset Albie more is a perceived slight against his father when he attends the professor's lecture (Albie's kind of 'disorganised killer', says Nolan, is likely to have suffered abuse at the hands of a violent, drunken father). His fourth victim, a white, working-class quarry foreman, is guilty of nothing more than blocking Albie's path to the explosives he needs to complete his plan. For all his righteous rhetoric, Albie, it's clear, is somewhat less than the just, working-class avenger he paints himself to be, as Fitz, with his sharp eye for the phoney motive, is quick to realise: 'You're doing this for yourself, Albie, nobody else. No altruistic motive, no mission.'

73

All the same, Albie's false 'mission' claims one very significant prize, thanks to a serendipitous union of narrative and real world events. After the first series of *Cracker*, frustrated at being forever in Coltrane's shadow, Christopher Eccleston had announced his desire to move on. Knowing his departure would leave the series without one of its most successful performers and Fitz without his main antagonist, the production team – and McGovern – were keen to change his mind. In the end, McGovern tempted him to remain for one further story on the promise of writing him a truly grandstanding death scene. It's certainly that. DCI Bilborough's is *Cracker*'s most memorable death, its most unexpected and dramatically powerful, wholly overshadowing the explosive and similarly symbolic demise of the *Sun* journalist, Clare Moody (Beth Goddard), at the end of the story.

Bilborough's has all the appearances of a hero's death, which in some ways it is. Yet even so, in keeping with *Cracker*'s insistent

A hero's death: Bilborough

examination of the purity of motive, it begins with an act not of selfless heroism but of personal vendetta, a revenge for Albie's molestation of his wife. It is this abuse of his sexual property as much as his professional duty that prompts Bilborough's pursuit. And his fury and impetuosity cause him to neglect his training: he ignores his police radio, neither requesting back-up nor giving information about his actions. Nor, as he pursues Albie through winding back alleys, does he pay attention to his location. This confluence of negligence and recklessness, to a great degree, defines Bilborough as a character and as a policeman, and virtually ensures his death: his inability to identify his position critically delays the arrival of help.

Bilborough's violent end represents a kind of dramatic restorative justice for the families of the Hillsborough dead.[10] McGovern insists the near homonym of 'Bilborough' and 'Hillsborough' was entirely accidental (the character was, he says, named after one of his former lecturers). Nevertheless, Bilborough is the disaster's sacrificial victim. In his arrogance and his blindness to justice, he personifies the police attitudes that led to Hillsborough, and he pays for Hillsborough with his life.

The eventual confrontation between Fitz and Albie resembles a dramatic manifestation of McGovern's own divided response to the Hillsborough tragedy, with Albie the wrathful Hyde and Fitz the rational, humanist Jekyll. Indeed, many of *Cracker*'s interrogations enact a moral argument between opposing projections of the writer's polarised psyche – with Fitz standing for the 'civilised' self against the 'savage' (for example, the stammering Sean in 'To Say I Love You'), or for the bitter non-believer against the righteous Catholic (Father Michael in 'Brotherly Love'). The ability to recognise the underlying motive behind acts too readily dismissed as 'mad' or 'bad' is what unites Fitz and his creator, and carries the series beyond the generic simplicities of good versus evil. Ultimately, Fitz unmasks the selfish motive that lies beneath Albie's false crusade, but in the process, in 'To Be a Somebody' as in almost all of *Cracker*'s stories, he reveals a basic and profoundly felt injustice. It is this that gives the series, at its best, much of its poignancy: while it never shirks from condemning the crime, it insists that we attempt to understand the criminal.

75

4 Grief Is Delicious

When it comes to murder, Fitz tells Bilborough during their first encounter in 'The Mad Woman in the Attic', 'you need someone who knows what they're doing, and I *do* know what I'm doing'. This is, in effect, a job application, but the swagger is typical of Fitz. But it is also something of a declaration of intent on the part of the series and its writer: where other TV crime drama stands back from a serious appraisal of murder, its cruelty and its pain, *Cracker* will not flinch.

We're used to death structuring a narrative: it has long been the familiar mode of many of our favourite stories, from *Hamlet* to Hammett. And murder has been a major component of most of Britain's more successful TV police dramas, even those which generally looked to more everyday crime – robbery, violence – for their stories. PC George Dixon (Jack Warner) famously died before he even made it to television, some twenty minutes into Ealing's *The Blue Lamp* (1950). The patrol units that gave *Z Cars* its name were put together in response to the murder of an officer on duty ('Four of a Kind', tx. 2/1/1962). And if early crime dramas reflected a time when murder was considered rare, by the early 1990s it was possible to see several murders on television on any evening of the week. TV writers were making a killing out of killing, and while the occasional scene of a weeping relative might be employed for extra dramatic effect, seldom were viewers troubled with the enduring emotional impact of death.

What's striking about *Cracker* is its attention to death's social and psychological ripples. McGovern's *Cracker* investigates death with

Driven by grief:
Craven in *Edge of Darkness*

Mrs Palmer in
Twin Peaks

77

a rare determination. Grief becomes a key narrative motor, just as it is in *Hamlet*, or to take two examples closer to *Cracker* in time and genre, in *Edge of Darkness*, whose hero, Craven (Bob Peck), becomes embroiled in a nuclear conspiracy as part of his personal investigation into the murder of his daughter, or in *Twin Peaks*, which is powered in its early episodes by the impact of Palmer's death on her small community. Crucially, it is in response to his own bereavement – the murder of his student Jacqui Appleby (Louise Downie) in 'The Mad Woman in the Attic' – that Fitz redirects his energies to 'cracking' crime. And it is his reaction to her death that first reveals the vulnerability and humanity that underlie his overbearing swagger.

Cracker's unique take on mortality stems in part from Neal's and McGovern's intent to examine the real consequences of crime, to remove the varnish of glamour that the media, whether in fiction or reportage, tends to apply. Certainly, some of the series' most powerful and memorable moments are those which express the enormity of a life ended: the death of Bilborough in 'To Be a Somebody', Fitz's counselling of the parents of young Timothy Lang in 'One Day a Lemming Will Fly' and his own response to the death of his mother in 'Brotherly Love'. McGovern cites approvingly George Orwell's description of death in his essay, *A Hanging*: 'one mind less, one world less' (McGovern, 2007a). But more than that, in McGovern's *Cracker*, bereavement is a core aspect of what we must consider almost a theory of criminal psychology.

Bereavement is a crucial component of most, if not quite all, of *Cracker*'s crimes. Hennessy, the real killer in 'Mad Woman' has recently lost his mother; Albie in 'To Be a Somebody' is driven to kill partly by the desire to revenge the dead of Hillsborough, but more by his overwhelming grief at the death of his father; Maggie Harvey in 'Brotherly Love' has for many years nursed her rage following the 'murder' of her unborn child in an abortion; and Beck's slow unravelling, decline and (literal) fall begins with his bottomless grief and guilt at Bilborough's death. And it is precisely this terrain of grief and emotional torment that calls for Fitz's unique skills.

Fitz's bold engagement with death is in stark contrast with the reaction of other professionals we meet along the way: the scene-of-crime expert who excitedly describes the murder as 'an absolute bloody classic' and poses for a photograph beside the bloodstains on the train carriage wall ('for the album'); the police officers who evade or bungle the awkward task of breaking the news of death to the family of the victim, then vent their frustration on the first available suspect; the pathologists who treat the dead as scientific curiosity or fascinating enigma; and the fellow psychologist who jokes of serial killers collecting their victims' body parts like sticks of rock as souvenirs.

It's a personal encounter with death that brings Fitz into his
new relationship with the Manchester police. The body whose
discovery coincides with his theatrical lecture belongs to his student,
Jacqui Appleby. Fitz is already emotionally vulnerable following the
exit of his wife and daughter, but it's clear that he was particularly fond
of Jacqui: later, in his interrogation of the amnesiac suspect, he speaks
vividly of her youth, beauty and intelligence; the video recording he
finds in Jacqui's bedroom captures the two of them together at the
university, with Fitz clearly relaxed and enjoying her company.
While there's no indication that there was ever a physical relationship
between Fitz and Jacqui, it's evident that he felt a powerful attachment
to her. She is perhaps a daughter substitute (a parallel with Emma
Craven in *Edge of Darkness*), rather than a lover. His initial response to
Jacqui's death is a very human, and arguably very British one – he
retreats to a private place (the loo) and weeps, hiding his grief from his
teenage son.

79

Furtive grief: Fitz absorbs the news of Jacqui's death

This response is characteristic of a society for which death, and our emotional response to it has, as Philippe Ariès argues, become something 'shameful and forbidden' (Ariès, 1976: 81, 85). In 1965, anthropologist Geoffrey Gorer complained that while old taboos surrounding sexuality in Britain had begun to retreat since Victorian times, a new and similarly damaging cultural repression of death and bereavement had emerged as if in their place:

> Today it would seem to be believed, quite sincerely, that sensible, rational men and women can keep their mourning under control by strength of will or character so that it need be given no public expression, and indulged, if at all, in private, as furtively as if it were an act of masturbation.
> (Gorer, 1965: 111)

This provocative analogy brings us back to Fitz, in his own grief, retreating to the lavatory and shutting the door in the face of his son. And yet, though this initial personal response might resemble shame, Fitz's professional and philosophical instincts tell him that grief and pain, like sexuality and anger, are intrinsic to humanity, that to repress them is to deny an essential part of ourselves.

This determination to confront death was a deliberate element of *Cracker* from the start. 'One of the rules of [*Inspector*] *Morse* was that the camera never went into the autopsy room,' notes Gub Neal (Crace, 1995: 23); *Cracker* would not permit such self-censorship – an adult audience, Neal and McGovern felt, not only could but *should* face death in all its brutality and finality.

Just as the first *Prime Suspect* used the setting of an autopsy room to demonstrate its protagonist's level-headedness in the face of death by comparison with a queasy male subordinate, the first of *Cracker*'s several autopsy scenes, in 'The Mad Woman in the Attic', shows Jane Penhaligon confounding expectations that she will show weakness, while her boss, DCI Bilborough, whose own youth and inexperience is a recurring issue, appears more troubled.

But the more significant opposition in the scene is that between Fitz and the pathologist (Paul Copley), between an essentially materialist attitude to death and the body and an idealist, religious one. The pathologist is eloquent in his disquisition on the beauty of the human body – 'the intricacy, the genius. No accident this – it's the work of an almighty God.' Fitz's dissent is concise (expressed in just three of his five words in the scene) but eloquent; he *radiates* scepticism. Crucially, of course, he knew the victim, and her death had a significant impact on him. For Fitz, her body, devoid of life, is little more than a husk. For the pathologist, the body itself is a miracle, evidence of God's grand design. For the detectives, professional detachment provides something of a shield. Fitz allows himself no such armour, exposing himself to the reality of his former student's death in its physical manifestation, to the indignities to her body during the autopsy and to the painful details of her last moments. Yet however uncomfortable he might be in the face of such pain, he retains sufficient distance to leave his analytical powers unimpaired. It is Fitz who, responding to the pathologist's observation that the shaving of the girl's pubic hair was exacted with 'tender, loving care', spots the forensic implication: 'two blades'.

In 'To Say I Love You', following the murder of his colleague DS Giggs, DS Beck loses his temper with another, female, pathologist (Rose English), who repeatedly refers to the dead policeman as 'the victim'. 'He's not "the victim",' insists Beck, 'he's Giggs. He's a policeman called Giggs, right? . . . This is no bloody civilian.' Leaving aside the implication that a 'civilian' might not deserve similar respect, Beck's anger is understandable: the pathologist's depersonalisation of his colleague is, to him, insensitive and disrespectful (this is one of several instances calling into question the way in which professionals deal with the bereaved). The dispassionate professionalism we expect the police to show at all times is hard to sustain when it comes to a murdered colleague and friend. And yet, as we see repeatedly in *Cracker*, without such detachment, the pursuit of true justice is undermined. Beck's outburst is less a healthy expression of grief than a manifestation of a characteristic hot-headedness that makes him a singularly bad policeman – a point reinforced in the subsequent scene, in which he organises the dawn arrest, without authority and without evidence, of an entirely spurious 'suspect'.

The inability to cope with grief is a recurring shortcoming in *Cracker*'s male survivors. Their repressed emotions typically lead to either anger or near-complete withdrawal (or, as with Albie, both). The exploration of gender difference in reactions to death is one of a number of ways in which the series foregrounds the 'problems' of masculinity. Whereas Mrs Appleby (Kika Markham) in 'The Mad Woman in the Attic' is articulate in her emotional expression, her husband (John Grillo) displays archetypal middle-class reserve. He is protective of his wife, but in a way that strongly implies that he is uncomfortable with and suspicious of her visible pain. In 'One Day a Lemming Will Fly', Mr Lang, father of the murdered Timothy, enacts his grief in the form of a terrifying wrath against the (innocent, as it turns out) suspect Cassidy, whose flat he attacks with an excavator; Tom Carter, husband of rape victim Catherine in 'Men Should Weep', similarly vents his fury against an innocent suspect, leaving the man hospitalised. Mr Barnes (Roger Sloman), father of the kidnapped Joanne in 'The Big Crunch', is so reticent on the police's first visit (when he is apparently completely absorbed in a televised boxing match while his anxious wife answers questions) that he briefly becomes a suspect; when Joanne later dies in hospital, however, his grief literally brings him, sobbing, to his knees, pathetically wrapping his arms around his wife's (Ellie Haddington) legs – he is simply not equipped to deal with the force of the emotion.

Fitz's response to his own grief could not be more different: he welcomes and embraces it, almost to the point of self-indulgence. 'Grief's delicious,' he tells Judith, 'Life's boring, banal. And then a parent dies, and at last there's a genuine emotion, a profound emotion. And you savour it. It's delicious.' Delivered through tears as he absorbs the death of his mother, it's a striking and affecting speech, and one it's hard to imagine coming from the lips of any other television character, or from the pen of any television writer other than Jimmy McGovern. It is another indication of the way in which Fitz embodies 'feminine' traits (emotional expressiveness, articulacy, sensitivity) as well as 'masculine' ones (rationality, intellectual competitiveness, aggression, self-destructiveness), but it is also a legacy of his Celtic working-class roots.

McGovern is drawn, by background and temperament, to exactly those 'genuine emotions' that the British character – at least by historical reputation – tends to repress, which, along with his Irish heritage, helps to explain his attraction to more emotionally expressive Celts:

> I've often felt that that's the Celtic working class – that they know passion and emotion, and they know when it's right, they know when it's genuine, and they suspect logic, because that logic tells you that you pay the poor less to make them work hard and pay the rich more. Logic is theirs, passion and emotion are ours, and we'll be the judge of when it's genuine or not. (McGovern, 2007a)

This passion and emotion is what gives McGovern's Liverpool, with its large Irish Catholic population, much of its character. But it can puzzle or infuriate outsiders, particularly those of the Southern media class who venerate a classical English emotional reticence. Attacks most often come from the political right, irritated by Liverpool's continuing tradition of trade union activism and its history of electing far-left local councillors, though it was the liberal *Observer* which printed Jonathan Meades' diatribe against the 'Liverpudlianisation of Britain': a 'no-holds-barred self-pity dressed as grief, self-congratulatory sentimentalism, an affirmation of itself through the appropriation of cosmetic Celtism' (Meades, 1997). Old stereotypes of lazy, dishonest Scousers have been joined by charges of a 'victim mentality'. In 2004, Tory frontbencher Boris Johnson was obliged to make a public apology to the city after a leader in the *Spectator* (16 October) accused Liverpudlians of a 'disproportionate convulsion of grief' over the death of Ken Bigley, the engineer from the city kidnapped and murdered in Iraq.

Coping – and
not coping –
with grief:
Mr and Mrs
Appleby

Mrs Lang

Mr Barnes

Albie

Catriona
Bilborough

85

Fitz

Characteristic of such attacks are disparaging allusions to Hillsborough (the dead were hardly in the ground before Edward Pearce, in *The Times*, declared Liverpool 'world capital of self-pity' (Pearce, 1989)), and a repetition of the old fallacies about the 'real' blame for the disaster. The *Spectator* leader's ignorance was demonstrated not only by its reference to the 'drunken fans ... who mindlessly tried to fight their way into the ground' – an interpretation of events specifically dismissed by Lord Justice Taylor – but also by his claim that the police had become a 'convenient scapegoat': a view not even the South Yorkshire police would dare express publicly. The leader worried of England's descent into 'mawkish sentimentality', as if fearing that Celtic emotional expression might somehow 'infect' the rest of the country. Faced with such vitriol, it isn't hard to understand why Liverpudlians might feel victimised. Representing the city can be something of a minefield, even for natives – one reason why McGovern preferred to set *Cracker* in Manchester rather than in his home city (McGovern, 2007a).

86   The fallout of Hillsborough is liberally scattered through McGovern's *Cracker*. It is at the root of McGovern's distinctive fusion of grief and anger. It is discernible in every injustice, in every grieving parent. It was Hillsborough that taught McGovern that grief may as easily tear a family apart as bring it together, just as Albie's marriage collapses a month after the tragedy and Mrs Appleby talks of leaving her husband 'once it's all over, and she's buried'. And there are more oblique references: Hale, the Lancashire suburb that is the scene of 'To Say I Love You''s explosive denouement, is where McGovern and his wife were when they first learned of the disaster. And it finds its purest expression in Albie's grief and anger.

By contrast with the painful, lingering death of Albie's father, Fitz's mother dies a fairly conventional modern death – in hospital after a stroke, from which she never regains consciousness. It is, then, Fitz's luxury to 'savour' his grief. There is no injustice, no incredulity; the rules of the universe remain intact. Her death, in old age, is part of the natural order. Such luxury, though, is denied to *Cracker*'s other survivors, whose relatives die brutal and premature deaths defying rational explanation, and for whom there is, as the title of one self-help book for survivors puts it, 'No Time for Goodbyes'.

The emotions unleashed by murder are powerful and frightening, even for professionals, as psychiatrist Colin Murray Parkes, at the forefront of the study and treatment of bereavement for more than forty years, notes:

> From the point of view of the therapist, families who have been traumatised by murder can be a daunting prospect. We easily feel overwhelmed by their grief and helpless in the face of their helplessness. The sheer enormity of the outrage that has been committed against them may be hard for us to bear, and it is tempting for us to distance ourselves from their suffering. (Parkes, 1993: 52)

For the police, without a therapist's training or skills of empathy and detachment, the responsibility to inform relatives of a violent death is an onerous one. This is the burden that invariably falls upon DS Penhaligon: 'You're good at that kind of thing,' explains Bilborough; 'I've had plenty of practice,' she sighs in reply.

Penhaligon may resent this duty, but she is demonstrably far better equipped to handle it than her male colleagues. As the Langs wait for news of their missing son in 'One Day a Lemming Will Fly', Beck, on the telephone, learns that a shoe has been found in the woods. 'What size shoe did he take?' he asks the anxious parents. This 'slip of the tongue' earns him a filthy look from Penhaligon, and he deserves it: his clumsy use of the past tense confirms the Langs' suspicion that their child is believed dead. After the body is found, Bilborough, having insisted that he will be the one to break the bad news, freezes, forcing Penhaligon to take over.

Fitz, though, is unflinching in the face of such challenges. His counselling of Timothy's parents occupies nearly five minutes of screen time, roughly a tenth of the episode – an unusually long time to hold up the action in a crime drama. But it establishes Fitz as a man of rare compassion and emotional courage. He anticipates their separate feelings of guilt and offers them understanding and acceptance: 'Guilt soon goes. Grief remains. But grief is your friend. It lets you mourn, remember, cry.' He is neither daunted nor overwhelmed; he has what it takes to confront the 'sheer enormity of the outrage' perpetrated against the Langs. The disparity with Bilborough could not be more stark, a point reinforced by Penhaligon, whose words of admiration for Fitz ('I thought you were brilliant in there') almost precisely invert her condemnation of her superior ('I thought you were a gobshite in there, sir').

Uniquely, for Fitz, the grief of the relatives is understood not just as a by-product of the crime – an uncomfortable distraction from the 'real' business of the investigation – but as an imperative; to him, the removal of impediments to grieving becomes an urgent task of the investigation. Though his initial animus is personal, his formal involvement with the police in 'The Mad Woman in the Attic' is prompted by Anne Appleby's complaint: 'I want to grieve for my daughter, and I can't because he's [the suspect's] in the way. I want him out of the way. Forgotten. I want to be able to grieve.' Unlike the police, Fitz is not content for the family to be pushed to the periphery.

Getting 'him out of the way' is more difficult than Mrs Appleby imagines; even the simple act of burying her daughter requires, in effect, the accused's consent, for the Defence has the right to demand an independent autopsy of the victim, and the body itself becomes, from the moment of death, the property of the Crown. Paul Rock, surveying the legal and bureaucratic minefield which families of murder victims are forced to negotiate, judges this loss of control 'one of the most potent symbolic assaults suffered by families in the wake of murder and manslaughter' (Rock, 1998: 76). So it was for the families of the Hillsborough dead. It is Penhaligon who explains this uncomfortable truth to the Applebys, but despite her evident sympathy, she and the police are powerless. Fitz, in his own mind as much the Applebys' envoy as the police's consultant, makes his own intervention, bringing the family's concerns into the interrogation room in an emotive plea to the suspect's humanity:

I've been to the house, twice. Met the parents. Can you imagine what you've put them through? It's not grief: grief is a process. They can't even begin that process thanks to you. It's desolation – cold, bleak, numb desolation. The daughter they loved is down in the morgue, in a refrigerated cupboard. Let them bury her. They have to bury her. People will say, 'He was a killer, he was a butcher, but he did one decent thing – he confessed so they could bury their daughter.' It's the last decent thing you can do. Please. *Please.*

There's maybe more than a touch of self-righteousness about his claim to speak for the parents, and a sense that his plea is, to an extent, another weapon in his interrogative arsenal. But however preachy or sanctimonious his speeches, Fitz is *at the same time* making the case for the wronged, for what is objectively right. In other words, it's not *why* he says what he says that matters, but the fact that he says it at all. Doing the right thing, irrespective of motive, is, in McGovern's world, as good as it gets.

While Fitz is empathetic in the face of grief, his opinion of society's attitudes to death is altogether more cynical: 'I had this idea: a soap opera, right, and all the actors – not the characters, mind you, all the actors – are convicted murderers. Fifteen million viewers, all of them women, no problem. All drooling at the mouth.'[11]

Fitz, in the wake of the first of Judith's walk-outs, outlines this provocative pitch to Kelly in 'Mad Woman', as the two return from a futile journey to meet the latter's 'wife' (who, we discover, has merely taken a shine to his photograph on TV). Kelly is not slow to see where Fitz is coming from. 'I'm sure she'll come back to you,' is his pitying response. But Fitz is merely riffing on a favourite theme: Sex and Death, Death and Sex. He offers another variant in 'To Say I Love You':

Do you remember the soldiers coming back from the Falklands? Remember all those women that lined the quays, waving their knickers and their bras in the air? Patriotism? No – lust. Some of those men had killed, and those women wanted them.

Death, he is fond of saying, is 'the finest aphrodisiac in the world'. And *Cracker*'s second story, 'To Say I Love You' provides the most explicit proof of his hypothesis.

In Sean, McGovern created the most overtly autobiographical of *Cracker*'s antagonists. Like the young Jimmy, Sean is almost completely unable to engage in 'normal' speech. And like his creator's former self, he achieves fluency only in song (a field in which he has found some measure of success, as his collection of karaoke trophies testifies), or in anger. With the techniques he has learned in speech therapy he can, with patience, communicate. But the speaker, he says, is not him but 'some dickhead'; anger allows him fluency without compromising his identity.

Tina enters Sean's life like an answer to a prayer, as if conjured out of the night by Sean's song. Their connection is immediate and absolute. It is Tina's near-telepathic ability to complete his sentences that earns her Sean's undying loyalty – she eases the burden of communication, offering him an escape from his suffocating isolation. In gratitude for that release, Sean will do anything.

Tina and Sean might describe their romance with typical adolescent hyperbole ('We love each other more than two people have ever loved each other'), but in a sense beyond the cliché, they really do complete each other. Just as she is his voice, Sean gives full expression to Tina's previously impotent rage. Sean's violent temper becomes the perfect means for the enacting of Tina's fantasies of power and revenge.

'To Say I Love You' is the most self-consciously *noir*ish of *Cracker*'s stories. It begins at night on a lonely street, and much of what follows take place at night. The action unfurls in smoky bars, rainy alleys and squalid flats; cars feature prominently. Emotions are exaggerated, and there is a powerful sense of a black, looming fate. The scarlet-lipsticked Tina resembles a sexually manipulative *femme fatale* in the mould of those incarnated by Barbara Stanwyck in *Double Indemnity* (1944) or Lana Turner in *The Postman Always Rings Twice* (1946). With its doomed-young-couple-on-the-run theme, the story of Tina and the hotheaded Sean follows a path cut by *They Live by Night*

The finest aphrodisiac in the world: Sean and Tina

(1948) and, especially, *Gun Crazy* (1950). But it is two later films, both associated with Hollywood's renewal in the late 1960s and early 1970s, and both combining *film noir* themes with elements borrowed from the Western and the road movie, that provide the story with its most direct points of reference.

  While Sean and Tina's murderous double act might inspire memories of an earlier Manchester couple, Ian Brady and Myra Hindley, in Tina's mind, their relationship quickly takes on the colour of the rebel outlaw story of Bonnie and Clyde, or at least of Arthur Penn's 1967 film of their exploits. Like Bonnie, she feels a rush of sexual excitement when she witnesses her first murder ('8.9 on the Richter Scale, mass evacuation of California time,' as Fitz imagines their post-homicidal sex), and it is to re-experience this rush that she urges Sean on to further murder, deliberately stoking his sexual jealousy to build his anger ('he's coming to screw me, Sean,' she reminds him when she senses his uncertainty about killing DS Giggs). 'I've got a man who's killed for me,' she subsequently boasts. As she says it, it sounds like a gift, a sacrifice. But the sacrifice, of course, is not Sean's.

Like Bonnie (Faye Dunaway) with her mythmaking poetry, Tina builds for herself and Sean a vivid false reality in which the matchless intensity of their love for one another ('if we're separated from each other, we'll die') justifies murder as 'self-defence'. One irony of Penn's film is that for all of Clyde's (Warren Beatty) allure, he is a virgin, ignorant and insecure about sex, who leaves Bonnie unsatisfied and frustrated. Similarly, after the second murder, of DS Giggs, Sean fails to deliver the rewards that Tina hoped for; instead of celebrating with sex, he sits alone in the bath, washing off the blood. Afterwards, she bandages his injured wrist: she is becoming more a mother than a lover (to reinforce the point, the scene echoes an earlier one in which Fitz's mother applies antihistamine to a wasp sting on his hand).

The other clue to Tina and Sean's movie fantasies emerges when the police raid Tina and Sean's abandoned flat, where a poster for Terrence Malick's 1973 film *Badlands* adorns one wall. Whereas Penn's *Bonnie and Clyde* explores its murderous protagonists' self-mythology in a way that appears celebratory, *Badlands* offers an altogether more complex, detached appraisal. It too is based on real-life events, in this case Charles Starkweather's late-1950s killing spree across Nebraska and Wyoming with his underage girlfriend Caril Ann Fugate. Malick's film is more self-evidently fictionalised, renaming its killers and shifting the events to the 'Badlands' of Dakota. Kit (Martin Sheen) is a callous, conscienceless killer, who commits murder with a shrug. Holly (Sissy Spacek), his young girlfriend and the story's narrator, is a listless dreamer, whose diary records her lover's actions without emotion. There is no attempt to imbue their acts with either glamour or romance; instead the film coolly notes Kit's elevation to media celebrity, a role that he, like Bonnie and Clyde, enthusiastically embraces.

The lesson of *Badlands* is that, in a society fixated with death, the notoriety gained by murder is as sure a route to celebrity as effort and talent – and a much easier one. While Tina imagines herself and Sean through the distorting lens of *Bonnie and Clyde*, the reality is closer to *Badlands*' Kit and Holly: tawdry, selfish and infantile. In one of his most ruthlessly effective rhetorical displays, Fitz smashes her illusions of romance by dissecting the iconic death scene of her outlaw heroes:

> I wept buckets. I wept buckets. I thought it was one of the worst moments in the entire history of Hollywood. I wept buckets for all the victims, and all the families of the victims. You see, I've been to their homes, Tina, I've seen it. I've seen what violent death does to a family. I've seen the grief and the numbness and the bitterness. I've seen them trying to imagine what they went through in their last moments. I've seen that kind of grief, you stupid little bitch, and it's always caused by empty-headed, self-centred, sentimental little pieces of shit like you.

The agents of law are not immune to the opportunity for celebrity that a murder investigation offers. In *Badlands*, Kit's captors vie for mementoes of their brush with the legend. In 'To Say I Love You', Tina and Sean's first murder attracts the interest of the 'Lenny Lion' chat show, and Fitz is chosen over an envious Bilborough to appear. Fitz uses his platform to decry the host and his audience: 'You're nosey, you're voyeuristic, you get turned on by suffering.' The charge, we realise, is just as applicable to us, the viewers. (McGovern, of course, is having his cake and eating it here, as he would probably admit – he, after all, is the one offering us murder and suffering in the name of entertainment.) But Fitz, too, is unable to resist the lure of performance, and ends up revealing his profile despite Bilborough's explicit request to withhold it.

'One Day a Lemming Will Fly' offers us another potent representation of the sex–death axis. The sequence begins with a woman running, apparently in terror, through moonlit woods, with a man in close pursuit. The chase echoes an earlier scene in which we see a young boy running through similar terrain; in both scenes there is a clear implication of threat (though we never see the boy's pursuer), with a strong hint in the second of a sexual element. When the couple reach a clearing, however, we discover that the woman is not a victim but a willing, even dominant, participant. But their passionate embrace is broken when the woman looks up and sees the body of the previously

93

seen boy hanging from a branch. This is a classic slasher film scenario –
particularly in the way the adulterous couple are 'punished' for their
sexual transgression – and one of a handful of scenes dotted through the
series that actively employ the tropes of the horror film.

The most striking of these are found in the particularly dark
pair of stories that close the McGovern era, 'Men Should Weep' and
'Brotherly Love'. After an opening sequence which, like Albie's shaved
head, recalls Martin Scorsese's *Taxi Driver* (with Fitz and a cab driver
travelling Manchester's mean streets while prostitutes and 'reclaim the
night' protesters battle it out, and one woman flashes her breasts at Fitz
through the cab window),[12] 'Brotherly Love' presents us with a semi-
comic 'old dark house' scenario. As the cab approaches a huge, dark
building, a shadowy form twitches a curtain at an upstairs window.
The building is a psychiatric hospital; the inmate (seemingly the only
one) is Jimmy Beck, recovering from a breakdown following his

94

Old dark house: Fitz visits Beck in the mental hospital

confrontation with Penhaligon, and the extended encounter between him and Fitz takes place in a large wood-panelled room bathed in gothic shadow.

But the most shockingly 'horrific' sequences of both stories, in ways that mirror one another, play freely with the iconography of the genre: lone women in peril, sexual threat, stairways (signifying the journey into an unknown space/the unconscious mind). In 'Men Should Weep', Deborah Wiley (Claire Hackett), wife of DSS official Andrew (Andrew Readman), returns home to find the back door open (the classic signal of an invading presence); her search for her missing cat (see, for example, *Alien*, 1979) leads her to venture recklessly *upstairs* (the shot of her ascent from above recalls *Psycho* (1960), while the slow-motion reinforces the sense of looming threat), where Floyd is waiting with his nightmarish mask and knife, like the villains of the *Halloween* (from 1978) and *Friday the 13th* (from 1980) series. The scarred black mask not only manifests the black side of Floyd's racial identity and the physical scarring that marks his body, it also recalls the burned face of *A Nightmare on Elm Street*'s (1984) Freddy Krueger (Robert Englund). Later, Andrew returns home to find water pouring through the kitchen ceiling, and is delayed in his journey upstairs by the police at the door. Wise and PC Skelton try unsuccessfully to prevent him entering the bathroom and seeing the body of his murdered wife – the sequence

95

Floyd in his 'slasher' mask

An image of true horror: Denise gets a bloodbath

has the feel of an urban myth of the kind liberally plundered by horror film narratives. We don't see the victim's body, though we can picture it well enough in the expressions of her husband and the two policemen.

96   'Brotherly Love', meanwhile, presents us with an image of true horror (in another 'old dark house': a run-down apartment block), when prostitute Denise (Polly Hemingway) is deluged in blood from the ceiling above, signifying the gruesome scene that awaits upstairs (the corpse of her friend, Paula (Irene Marot)), just as the cascading water hints at the wife's fate in 'Men Should Weep'. The spectacle of the blood-drenched Denise recalls the climax of *Carrie* (1976) and an even more strikingly similar scene in budget-horror auteur Norman J. Warren's lesser-known *Terror* (1978). Notably, this time we are not spared the sight of Paula's body; instead we are confronted with an image that is the series' grisliest since that nightmarish train carriage in 'Mad Woman'. The defilement of the bodies of Paula and the other victims – the insertion of a chisel into their vaginas before or after death – expresses the killers' (David Harvey and his wife Maggie) violent disgust at sex (or at least prostitution) more vividly than almost anything offered up by the classic 'slasher' narrative.

Nevertheless, while later TV crime dramas (notably the baroquely gothic *Messiah*), seemed intent on extending what was permissible on the small screen, *Cracker* is more cautious than its reputation in some quarters allows. The bloody railway carriage (and the title) of 'The Mad Woman in the Attic' might suggest a gruesome horror excursion: certainly Hennessy's weapon of choice (a cut-throat razor) and his 'Sweeney' soubriquet connect him to the slasher of urban myth and movie nightmare. But the drama that follows steps back from the gore to take a very different path. In 'To Say I Love You', Tina and Sean's fantasies of Bonnie and Clyde glamour are very deliberately contrasted with the prosaic brutality of their killings – a brick over the head for their first victim, a metal bar for their second. But most of *Cracker*'s murders happen either off screen – as they do in 'Mad Woman', 'Lemming', 'Men Should Weep', 'True Romance' and 'White Ghost' – or at a discreet distance, as in Jean McIlvanney's (Ruth Sheen) brutal killing in 'Brotherly Love'. Where we are brought up close to the murder itself, as with the deaths of Ali (Badi Uzzaman) and Bilborough in 'To Be a Somebody', it is ugly and shocking; there is none of the grisly celebration characteristic of the slasher film, or what Gorer (1965) described as the 'pornography of death'. In *Cracker*, as Fitz reminds Father Michael in 'Brotherly Love', 'all murder is brutal'.

97

With the exception of Mrs Fitzgerald's, all of *Cracker*'s deaths are premature and painful. There are no clear descendants here of the Victorian and pre-Victorian 'good' death – at home in bed, attended by friends and family. The death of DCI Bilborough in 'To Be a Somebody', though, gives us something at least analogous. To paraphrase *Macbeth*, nothing becomes Bilborough's life like the leaving of it; in his final moments, the character achieves a nobility far beyond anything he has demonstrated in his professional life. It is, in a sense, a parody of a 'good' death: Bilborough dies in violence, alone, and takes his last breaths not in his bed but on a cold, wet pavement, yet his colleagues attend, gathered at the end of a radio line, hanging on his every word. Alone of *Cracker*'s victims to this point, he is afforded the privilege of a dying speech, and like a patriarch on his deathbed, his words convey imperatives that cannot be ignored: 'I want you to get this bastard, Jimmy, OK? For me and Catriona.'

Bilborough's failings as a policeman are forgotten – not just by (most of) the audience but, more importantly, by his colleagues – in the face of the courage and selflessness of his words, as he lies bleeding on the street: 'This is evidence: this is a dying man's statement. I know what a Defence lawyer will try to do. I'm of sound mind. I'm frightened, yeah – I don't want to die. I'm frightened, but I'm thinking straight.' These are the words of a man attending to the end to his duty: a hero's words. We should know by now, of course, not to expect a pure motive, least of all from a man looking death in the eye. And there is great humanity and pathos in Bilborough's final words, as his thoughts turn to his family. But the authority of his exhortation to Beck stems not from his superior rank, but exactly from the circumstances of its utterance. The ritual of death decrees that it is the solemn duty of the attendants to carry out the dying man's last wishes. Bilborough's is a *personal* demand: not an order but a direct appeal to 'Jimmy', and not to the collective police investigation.[13] It is a demand not for *justice* – for all of Albie's victims – but for *vengeance*, 'for me and Catriona'. And so it is taken by Beck, who, having apprehended Albie, quite clearly has something other than lawful justice on his mind.

There are more than thirty deaths scattered across *Cracker*'s eleven stories, but it is Bilborough's that casts the biggest shadow; we can measure its impact on each of his colleagues, and his ghost lingers until 'Brotherly Love' three stories later (and indeed, appears to materialise, in the shape of his hitherto unmentioned brother), before it is finally laid to rest with Beck's suicide. By comparison, Albie's murder of the *Sun* journalist, Clare Moody (and perhaps many others in the same explosion), fails to even register on an emotional level. In 'To Say I Love You', Tina, in a videotaped message, announces, 'We're going to kill a policeman. People think that's worse than killing an ordinary person.' It is a view that many don't share, including, presumably,

McGovern, but it is one that the weight of Bilborough's murder can only reinforce.

But if *Cracker* shows us anything, it is that *every* death is a tragedy for someone. In the classic detective fiction, death constitutes the beginning of the *mystery* – an intellectual challenge for the hero. So too, in *Cracker*, but the series never allows us to see death as anything so abstract. Death, here, is the beginning of the *pain* – not so much for the victim as for those left behind.

5 Faith of Our Fathers

Jimmy McGovern's first six stories for *Cracker* begin with Fitz's confession of rehearsing his father's death, and end with his burying his mother and celebrating the birth of his third child. The same two stories – 'The Mad Woman in the Attic' and 'Brotherly Love' – share an unusually detailed exploration of Catholicism and Catholic morality. In between, the series maintains an intense scrutiny of the family – Fitz's and many others – under duress, while continuing the relentless

examination of faith that distinguishes much of McGovern's work both before and since: *Traitors* (BBC, 1990); *Priest*; *The Lakes* (BBC, 1997–9); *Liam*; *Gunpowder, Treason and Plot* (BBC, 2004). McGovern honed his craft on the family sagas of *Brookside* (particularly the Catholic Grants) and has repeatedly filled his plots and his characters with the legacy of his Catholic upbringing and education. Paul Abbott, meanwhile, has his own reasons for a preoccupation with issues of family, which came into focus with the autobiographically inspired domestic chaos of his later hit *Shameless* (Channel 4, 2004–). His three *Cracker* stories for the most part step back from the big political, religious and social themes that characterised the McGovern era, focusing instead on more personal issues, in a way that perhaps reflects the differences between the two writers' respective backgrounds on *Brookside* and *Coronation Street*.

McGovern's schooling was, he says, straight out of *Portrait of the Artist as a Young Man*, James Joyce's classic evocation of a Catholic education in late nineteenth-century Ireland: 'I just love that novel. I so

identify with it' (Butler, 1995). He attended the Jesuitical St Francis
Xavier primary school and, after passing his eleven-plus exam,
graduated to the associated grammar school. The priests were brutal
and reactionary, beating the boys with whalebone and leather, while
McGovern's poverty marked him out for worse treatment than his peers
(Day-Lewis, 1998). It was, as he told Sue Lawley on BBC Radio 4's
Desert Island Discs in 1996, 'an absolutely horrendous school', and his
lifelong bitterness towards the Church started there. Even so, he retains
an abiding anger at the long history of persecution of British and Irish
Catholics, as embodied in his 'favourite' hymn, which has appeared
more than once in his work:

> Faith of our fathers, living still,
> in spite of dungeon, fire, and sword;
> [. . .]
> Faith of our fathers, holy faith!
> We will be true to thee till death.

101

In *I Confess* (1953), one of Alfred Hitchcock's more earnest
films, a Catholic priest (Montgomery Clift) hears about a murder in
confession and is therefore bound by the seal of the ceremony from
reporting it, even when he finds himself accused and his past mistakes
are painfully scrutinised in the courtroom. Hitchcock was drawing on
his Catholic background, just as Jimmy McGovern repeatedly draws on
his own: McGovern didn't need Hitchcock to tell him of the dramatic
potential of the confessional seal – or, indeed, of the torment of being
unable to speak.

The revelation of monstrous acts in confession is a favourite
McGovern device. In *Traitors*, his 1990 single drama about the
gunpowder plot, much of the narrative focus is on Father Henry Garnett
(Geoffrey Hutchings), a priest who becomes aware of the plot in
confession and is powerless to prevent or report it, and whose duty to the
Church overrides his loyalty to the state, even when he is tortured for his
supposed complicity. In *Priest*, Linus Roache's Father Greg endures a

more spiritual pain for his own moral compromises in surrendering to his homosexual desires, but more so for his inability to act when he learns in the confession box of the incestuous abuse of a teenage girl.

In 'Mad Woman in the Attic', Fitz's intimate knowledge of Catholicism alerts him to the fact of Kelly's own faith ('He's a Catholic grammar school boy, same as me, God help him'); Kelly's religious education has made its mark so deep that even near-total amnesia cannot erase it. Conversely, Bilborough's ignorance of the faith leads him to be duped by the anonymous 'priest' who reveals the whereabouts of a previously unknown victim and identifies Kelly as the killer, claiming that he heard about the murder in confession. Fitz, of course, recognises at once that the caller's willingness to divulge information supposedly heard in confession proves that he is no priest ('That's number one in the top twenty of sins – that's above buggering the Pope'), and must, therefore, be the killer. It is, in other words, precisely Fitz's status as a lapsed Catholic that equips him to solve the case.

In 'Brotherly Love', after murdering the prostitute Jean McIlvanney, David Harvey goes to his Catholic priest brother, Father Michael, speaking the formal words of the confession. The seal of confession bars Father Michael from talking to another of what he has heard, but it does not oblige him to advise his brother in the concealment of the crime as he does; family bonds reinforce religious ones in a way that morally compromises the otherwise apparently benevolent priest.

Elsewhere, Fitz's former faith expresses itself in his relentless pursuit of motive (pure and impure) and, more implicitly, in his understanding of confession as an unburdening of otherwise overwhelming guilt (as opposed to the police's altogether more functional definition) – it is this burden that Fitz offers to share with Cassidy in 'One Day a Lemming Will Fly'.

Another confession box scene appears in 'The Big Crunch', when the autistic Dean attempts to tell Father O'Ryan (Nicholas Blane) about the murder of Joanne Barnes; the confused and frightened Dean is, however, unable to speak, and runs from the box – just as, we can imagine, the young Jimmy McGovern might have done. The writer here, though, is not McGovern but Ted Whitehead. Whitehead's Dean is recognisably a version of the stuttering Sean (whose name he almost shares) from 'To Say I Love You', and it his communication deficit that renders him unable to prove himself innocent of Joanne's murder and, ultimately, drives him to suicide.

This device is just one example of the way Whitehead's story reshuffles structural and thematic elements of McGovern's earlier *Cracker* stories – obstacles to communication; the miscarriage of justice; the torturing grief unleashed by the death of a child; Fitz's lapsed Catholicism and his repurposing of Catholic notions of confession and absolution; gambling; society's disproportionate fear of child abuse (in a witty subplot which sees Fitz, innocently meeting Katie outside her school, accused of being a predatory paedophile; the irony is that the real danger lurks not outside the school gates but *inside* – albeit not the same school – in the form of headmaster Kenneth Trant (Jim Carter)).

It is Whitehead, not McGovern, who engineers Fitz's first face-to-face encounter with a servant of his former faith, as he and Penhaligon interview the priest Father O'Ryan about Joanne – herself a once-devout Catholic who was lured away from her Church by Kenneth. The meeting, however, has none of the fireworks we might have hoped for. This is a rather subdued Fitz, pacified by the recent promising turn of his relationship with Penhaligon. Fitz, perhaps mischievously, acknowledges their similarities ('we're both confessors'), while stressing, too, their differences: 'my job is to listen and understand', he tells the priest, 'your job is to listen and forgive – that must be even harder'. For his part, the priest is able to deduce Fitz's background, he tells him, 'because you're so serious in your mockery'. Their sparring is essentially good-natured, and the two men part with smiles.

That Father O'Ryan gets such a surprisingly easy ride from Fitz is partly a function of his role in the narrative: he is the 'good priest', who serves to oppose the 'bad priest', Kenneth Trant, headmaster, leader of the non-established Fellowship of Souls and seducer of troubled

103

The good priest:
Father O'Ryan

And the bad:
Kenneth Trant

104

Perverse ritual

young girls. Both men are intelligent and highly educated, but where O'Ryan is benevolent, compassionate, self-questioning but steadfast in his faith, Trant is manipulative, vengeful, corrupt and corrupting. The two men, though, inhabit parallel and mutually intelligible worlds: it is Father O'Ryan who informs Fitz and Penhaligon of Trant's predatory recruitment of girls from his school for his church.

Contact with Kenneth and the Fellowship's other leaders, all members of the Trant family – Kenneth's wife Virginia (Maureen O'Brien), his brother Michael (James Fleet) and Michael's wife Norma (Cherith Mellor) – appears to put Fitz temporarily at ease with his own faith, which seems benign in comparison with the Fellowship's hypocrisy and iniquity. With its emphasis on conspiratorial solidarity and its perverse ritual (the collective poisoning of Joanne and the mock-sacred markings adorning her naked body), the Fellowship's joint leadership – dominated by the overpoweringly charismatic Kenneth – resembles less a Christian group than a *coven*, a point emphasised by a shot from above of the four Trants sitting circled, hands joined in dark prayer.

In 'Brotherly Love', McGovern allows Fitz an altogether more two-fisted confrontation with his one-time faith. In a reversal of the series' now familiar interrogation/confession scenes, this one begins with Fitz's own confession to Father Michael, apparently a prelude to taking communion at his mother's funeral, and ends with him receiving absolution from the priest. Since Fitz has previously – and quite emphatically – refused to take communion, it seems that his approach to Father Michael is essentially an excuse to interrogate the priest, who Fitz suspects of murdering the second prostitute, Joyce (Sharon Percy), to remove suspicion from his brother, David.

It is a riveting contest between two formidable intellects, in which Fitz and the priest scrutinise one another's souls while engaging in profound discussion touching on matters theological (does absolution have meaning when the priest is morally tainted?) and moral (the ethics of prostitution). Also observable is a profound difference on matters metaphysical. 'You think I'm capable of that [murder]?', asks Father

105

Fitz takes communion

Michael, 'And yet you'd let me bury your mother?' 'She's dead,' responds Fitz angrily, 'You're going to put her in a hole in the ground tomorrow, that's all.' Fitz's attitude to death here, as in his exchange with the pathologist in 'The Mad Woman in the Attic', reveals just how far he has travelled from Catholic orthodoxy. Father Michael gives very nearly as good as he gets – 'You'll come back to us,' he sneers, 'when your body can't take the booze any more, or there's a cough you can't get rid of, or a lump that won't go away.'

However morally compromised he is by his abetting of his brother, Father Michael is no murderer; he is, within limits, a 'good priest', as his concern for his homeless parishioners demonstrates, aware of his own fallibility and that of his profession. 'I'm a celibate priest,' he tells Wise, 'there are one or two of us still around.' But the story's dissection of religion does not begin and end with Father Michael. At its heart is the 'virgin/whore' dichotomy that, for its critics, dominates Catholicism's representations of women. For all that Maggie Harvey contends that she and her husband enjoy 'a healthy sex life', Catholicism is the source of David's neurotic anxiety about female desire. The portrait of Maggie cradling a newborn child in the Harveys' living room is unmistakably a likeness of the Holy Mother and the infant Christ, while her sizeable brood (four living children) testifies to the inextricable association of sex and parenthood. David's predilection for acting out 'Shirley Temple' routines with prostitutes, meanwhile, indicates his confusion about sexual purity, while his grotesque defilement of his victim's body, inserting a chisel into her vagina, betrays his disgust. 'I knew you'd be Catholic,' Fitz tells him, 'Dressing up like Shirley Temple? Innocence, virginity – Catholicism.'

Catholicism, too, is behind the murderous campaign of Maggie Harvey, whose own hatred, coupled with her desire to free her husband, leads her to kill two more prostitutes and to attempt to kill a third. Rage at her husband's betrayal provides one explanation, exacerbated by the realisation that his spending on prostitutes left her family in poverty. But another source of Maggie's hatred is her own fundamentalist piety, a monstrous devotion that shocks even her priest/brother-in-law. The deep wound, nursed for some twenty years, is the abortion of her first child, and the failure of Father Michael – and through him the Church – to intervene to prevent her from carrying it out. 'I'm a good Catholic,' she protests, 'I believe. I go along to my priest ... and all I ask is that he protect the child growing in my womb.' Father Michael's version of Catholicism, which attempts to tailor the Church's moral absolutes to the realities of modern life, is altogether too liberal for Maggie. Her careful replication of David's murder – to the alarming detail of the chisel in the vagina – is indicative of more than exactitude (unlike her husband, we're told, Maggie inserts the chisel while the victim is still living); it is an expression of brutal moral judgment, and a revenge for the women's perceived role in the death of her unborn child. 'Whatever mess I made of them,' she tells Fitz, 'it was nothing compared to what they did to my baby.' In the end, though,

107

Maggie Harvey's unsisterly violence is an expression of a much more fundamental female instinct – she kills to protect her family, in the certain knowledge that without her efforts, her children will be left without their father (which, thanks to Beck's particular brand of justice, they are).

Both 'The Big Crunch' and 'Brotherly Love', then, explore the interface between faith and family in ways that accent the fault lines of both. But if other *Cracker* stories, including McGovern's, don't always express their religious themes so openly, a preoccupation with the functioning – and dysfunctioning – of family pervades the series. The integration of family storylines into crime drama is not, of course, an innovation in itself. PC George Dixon's daughter Mary was a regular character in *Dixon of Dock Green*, marrying her father's colleague, Andy Crawford; *Z Cars*, too, occasionally took its cameras into its police protagonists' living rooms. The handful of dramas led by female detectives – *Juliet Bravo*, *The Gentle Touch* (ITV, 1980–4) and *Prime Suspect* – have paid attention to their heroines' domestic arrangements, sharing a concern with their difficulties in sustaining healthy family relationships. The first *Prime Suspect* also explored the titular suspect's relationships with his wife and mother.

Still, the degree of attention paid to the domestic in *Cracker* marks it out as unusual for its genre. Judith and Mark appear in every story (save the Hong Kong-set 'White Ghost') and Katie in most, while storylines also feature Fitz's mother (Beryl Reid) and his brother, Danny; Bilborough's wife, Catriona, his son, Ryan, and, briefly, his brother, John; Wise's wife, Renee (Liz Estenson), and Beck's sister, Aileen (Aisling O'Sullivan). The parallel domestic and professional worlds, moreover, frequently collide: Bilborough's anxiety about the heavily pregnant Catriona clouds his judgment in 'One Day a Lemming Will Fly', while Judith's postnatal depression in 'Best Boys' means that Fitz has to take newborn Jimmy to work. The domestic arena, moreover, is not only the province of recurring characters: as we have seen, the focus on the suffering of survivors means that considerable screen time is devoted to the families of the victims and to the exploration of their complex and diverse experiences of grief and anger.

In almost every story, moreover, we are also introduced to the killer's family – only Sean ('To Say I Love You') mentions no family at all, while Cassidy's mother ('One Day a Lemming Will Fly') is mentioned but never seen. This serves the series' agenda of putting the crime and the criminals in a social context. Thus Tina's resentment ('To Say I Love You') has a visible target in her blind and dependent sister and bourgeois parents. Likewise, Albie's broken marriage is a factor in his descent into brutal rage and murder, the death of his father still more so.

With the exception of Hennessy ('Mad Woman') and Floyd ('Men Should Weep'), *Cracker*'s killers have no prior criminal history. Our encounters with their families normalise them in our eyes, helping us to see them as real people rather than evil 'monsters'. Floyd's family eat together at the table – a signifier of family unity in an age when such rituals are, we're told, dying out – and bicker in the way that even loving families do. We see David Harvey's dark side in his 'Shirley Temple' routine with Jean McIlvanney, but afterwards he visibly weakens as the prostitute harangues him over the money. And when he returns home to his crowded home we understand him as a man beaten down by mundane poverty. It is when the sanctity of his imperfect domestic life is threatened that the weak man transforms into a brutal killer. Similarly, in 'The Big Crunch', it is the threat that the pregnant Joanne poses to their family integrity, as well as to their fragile faith, that makes murderers of Kenneth and the other Trants.

'Men Should Weep', the climactic story of *Cracker*'s second series, is shaped around a nexus of families uniting, broken or being forced apart. Its three episodes depict a particularly momentous period for the Fitzgeralds, with the return of Judith to the family home after several months' absence and the revelation of her pregnancy. Quickly after, Judith discovers Fitz's affair with Penhaligon, a relationship that, he acknowledges, probably springs from the younger woman's desire for a substitute for her dead father. Woven into the same story are the christening of the orphaned Ryan Bilborough, and the tortured Jimmy Beck's overtures to the baby's mother, Catriona; the effect of rape on the

109

Happy families:
the Fitzgeralds with
newest addition

The Harveys

110

The Malcolms

Tina's parents

families of the victims, and the threat to the police 'family' of
Penhaligon's allegation of rape against her colleague.

The background to these stories is the serial rapist and, ultimately, killer, Floyd Malcolm, whose confused racial identity is born of his mixed-race parentage (exacerbated, perhaps, by the unexplained absence of his black father). 'Men Should Weep' features one of *Cracker*'s most unsettling conceits, the decision of a dark-skinned nine-year-old boy to sit in a bath of bleach, telling his white mother, 'I want to be like you.' McGovern explains that this happened to a boy who went to school with his son, but similar stories can be found elsewhere. Ngozi Onwurah's 1988 short film, *Coffee-Coloured Children*, shows a young girl attempting to lighten her skin with powdered bleach, while a young boy tries to scrub off his brown colour in the bath. In Yasmin Alibhai-Brown's book *Mixed Feelings*, actress Danielle Brown, sister of Spice Girl Mel B, recalls that in response to racial taunts as a schoolgirl, she would 'plaster my face with white powder to look like the other kids', though she stresses that she has no anxieties about her colour now (Alibhai-Brown, 2001: 104). McGovern, meanwhile, emphasises that 'I wasn't suggesting how ignoble it was for this black boy to be ashamed of his blackness. What I was saying was, this is what white society does to these black kids, particularly kids who've got black father, white mother' (McGovern, 2007b).

After an opening scene in which Fitz, in his new role as a radio therapist,[14] mischievously calls on listeners to steal from a local supermarket in response to its harsh treatment of an elderly shoplifter, the story's first episode cuts to the home of the Malcolm family. We begin with a close-up of youngest son Marvin (Alexander Newland), before cutting to a similar shot of his elder brother Floyd. As the third child, sister Bev (Julie Saunders), passes behind Floyd's shoulder, the camera pans and pulls back to reveal the final member of the family. Only now do we see that these three black children share a white mother (Rachel Davies). The subject of their conversation is another 'petty' crime, Floyd's decision to continue drawing unemployment benefit despite his job as a minicab driver, which his mother characterises as stealing. While Bev comes to Floyd's defence, Marvin abstains, more concerned with listening to Fitz's radio show. The arguments, then, are not precisely delineated by race, but it's notable that Mrs Malcolm has no allies. As Floyd gets up to answer the doorbell, the Malcolms fall silent, allowing us for the first time to hear the radio clearly. Over a close-up of Mrs Malcolm, the voice of a caller speaks the words, 'mother – bloody mother'.

This scene subtly prepares us for the moment when, under pressure from Fitz, Mrs Malcolm will symbolically abandon her son. Her interview (and the story's third episode) begins incongruously with Penhaligon's tearful recollection of a beating at the hands of her father, a memory brought up by her recent rape. After this emotive start, Fitz plays on Mrs Malcolm's latent guilt and anxiety, asking 'who turns a child into a monster if not the person who has most influence on them? And who is that person? His mother.' It is this provocation which elicits the account of Floyd's childhood encounter with the bath of bleach, after which she reveals her son's whereabouts.

Later, when he interrogates Floyd, Fitz taunts him with his mother's betrayal, chipping away at their familial bond, and finally provoking the son into declaring their essential difference: 'She told you 'cos she's white! [. . .] This guy's raping white women, yeah, women like her. When it comes down to it, it's her colour. It's her colour even before her own son!' Floyd's internalisation of this difference, is, we understand, the root of his drive to rape white women, having betrayed his ambivalence towards his blackness by first raping black women – as practice, suggests Fitz. As part of his interrogative strategy, Fitz relates the case of 'a patient' who can only have sex with other men's wives: he is, Fitz observes, symbolically 'screwing the other guy'. Fitz, surprisingly, fails to carry the analysis further: the obvious psychoanalytic interpretation of Floyd's behaviour is Oedipal: he is symbolically raping his mother by selecting 'women like her', perhaps as much as a punishment of his father (whose absence is strangely unexplained) as for her own unignorable difference.

Though he insists he is 'proud of his colour', Floyd's issues about his racial identity run deep, as reflected by his tendency to hide behind an assumed Jamaican accent – 'me like to spill I'm from Jamaica,' he tells the DSS official. This confusion is permanently etched on to his bleach-scarred skin, and expresses itself in his crimes, each one an act of revenge directed less at women than at the white men who have personally offended him and who stand for those whose persecution drove his young self to such a desperate measure. In his vengeance he adopts the role of the black sexual predator of paranoid white fantasy. 'What do you dread most?', he asks Fitz, 'You and every other white man? Your nice white wife getting raped by a big – and I mean *big* – black man.'

This theme is expressed early in episode one with taxi controller Tom's blue joke, which repeats the aged myth that black men have larger penises (Tom's unwillingness to tell this joke in front of Floyd points up the latter's outsider status and leads him to enact his revenge on Tom's wife, Catherine). The irony is that this scene follows one in which Floyd refuses to undress in front of girlfriend Trish (Ludmilla Vuli), explaining that 'You wouldn't like me when I'm naked'

113

– prompting us to speculate that he suffers anxieties about his endowment. Floyd's naked body thereafter becomes a source of fascination. At the time of his first arrest, he is in bed, and is still pulling his shirt over his bare chest as he is dragged into the street. The third time the police come for him, they find him in the shower at a friend's house. Behind the bathroom door, a glossy black-and-white photo depicts a hairless black man embracing a paler-skinned woman in a bath; the legend reads, 'IT'S A BLACK THING'. When Wise pulls back the curtain that conceals Floyd's naked form, Wise and Beck's eyes drift downwards, the camera following their gaze. Their fascination is mirrored by our own. We are intrigued to see the scarring we have heard about, but we also want to test the myth for ourselves. Desire and horror, then, combine in a single image, but while we see the ugly scarring on Floyd's buttocks and legs, his back remains turned to us. As the poster frustrates our desire by concealing what we really want to see, so we never get to see Floyd's 'black *thing*'.

Such intensive explorations of racial and sexual mythologies makes 'Men Should Weep' one of McGovern's most bracing stories, forcefully demonstrating his fearlessness in the face of the most troubling social issues. But while making highly effective drama, it also manifests some of the series' weaknesses. First, the brief presence of Floyd's lawyer (whose arrival interrupts Fitz's interrogation just as the suspect is about to confess) highlights the fact that her kind are wholly absent elsewhere in the series. This departure from reality is one that drew criticism from *Prime Suspect* creator Lynda La Plante, for one, and it's true that in the wake of the 1984 Police and Criminal Evidence Act, it was unimaginable that interrogations could routinely take place without the accused's legal representation being present. By the same token, though, the central tenet of *Cracker* – that a consultant forensic psychologist (particularly one so combative) could play such a dominant role in police investigations – is similarly questionable, and without that, there is no series. The balancing of strict verisimilitude with dramatic cohesion is part of the process of drama, and no police series, including *Prime Suspect*, is entirely innocent of such compromises.

It's a black
thing

Fascinated gaze

115

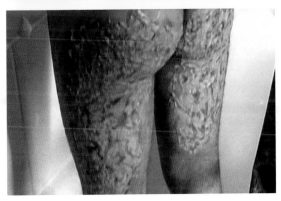

Desire and
horror

More serious concerns, however, arise from *Cracker*'s
representations of race. The story saw Granada's Manchester studios
picketed by feminist campaigners who argued that 'by making the main
rapist a black man, the programme diverts public concern about rape
into anger against black people' (*Independent*, 26 November 1994).
It's reasonable to respond that most of *Cracker*'s criminals are white, that
black rapists do exist and should therefore be dramatically permissible,
and that the story is devoted to understanding the social pressures that
might turn a troubled mixed-race boy into an adult predator. Moreover,
behind such criticism arguably lies the view that drama can only be
deemed socially responsible if it conforms to a particular representative
mode. But however studiously script and performances strive to make
Floyd a complex figure and to invite sympathy for his experiences of
racism, he remains another example of television's persistent
representation of black men as criminal and/or sexually predatory.
And Floyd is the only really fleshed-out black character in over twenty
hours of *Cracker*. While the series presents an altogether more positive
representation of black masculinity in the form of PC Skelton, this
defence is somewhat undermined by the fact that Skelton, however
sympathetically portrayed, is so underdeveloped. In 'Men Should Weep',
he has little role other than as an object of hostility for Floyd, just as, in
'To Be a Somebody', he is merely a focus for the skinheads' racism.

Floyd's *modus operandi*, targeting the partners of men who
have threatened him, finally leads him to Judith, and it is this threat that
appears to confirm Fitz in his recommitment to his marriage and family.
Fitz's ambivalence, however, is signalled in his response to the sight of
Floyd with his knife to Judith's throat: 'Go on, we've been married
twenty-odd years – I'm sick of her. Go on, kill her.' This is, of course, a
gambit to unsettle Floyd and buy time, during which Mark creeps
downstairs to disarm Floyd. But while Fitz, Judith and Mark
subsequently come together in a collective embrace, the underlying
tensions of Fitz's relationships with both wife and son remain unresolved.

Floyd might represent an absolute threat to the Fitzgeralds, but
a more sustained one comes in the form of Jane Penhaligon. Or rather,

Fitz and family:
Judith

Katie

117

... and Mark

two threats: for Penhaligon represents not just sexual temptation but an escape into work. 'I'm forty-five years old and I've finally discovered what I want to do with my life,' Fitz tells Judith in 'To Be a Somebody', 'I want to work with the police. When I'm doing that everything's fine. When I'm not doing that I get bored and depressed, things go wrong.' Judith, understandably, takes this badly. But although Fitz insists that he didn't mean to imply that he blames her, his work unmistakably becomes a means of evading the family responsibilities with which he seems so ill at ease. For every scene showing Fitz apparently comfortable in his domestic surroundings, there are two or more in which he seems awkward and out of place. Home is a disorientating place for Fitz, where he is frequently confronted by bewildering change. 'To Be a Somebody' alone confronts him with inept plumbers, an invasion of Mark's friends (to celebrate a birthday that Fitz had forgotten) and Judith's unexpected departure. Small wonder that Fitz's own bathroom becomes the scene for his apparent heart attack. Shortly before she leaves, Judith submits Fitz to a humiliating tour of the house to uncover his concealed booze, suggesting that, as Glen Creeber (2002) notes, he can only negotiate the house's unwelcoming territory with the comfort of a drink. In Judith's absence he quickly allows the house to degenerate into the kind of squalor for which he regularly berates Mark.

Narratively, Fitz's family serves as a recurring reminder of his inadequacy in traditional masculine roles – as husband, father, provider – an inadequacy that is most glaring when he is kept at bay from his police work, as he is in 'To Be a Somebody'. With the police, by contrast, he displays the competence and assurance which are a social hallmark of masculine professionalism. Or at least he starts that way. For as long as he can keep his two worlds apart, Fitz manages to cope, and even excel, professionally. As his relationship with Penhaligon develops, however, domestic and professional spheres creep towards one another, imperilling both.

For Fitz, of course, that relationship is one more manifestation of his middle-life flight from commitment. Penhaligon's own attraction,

118

though, is for some critics one of *Cracker*'s 'problems': that this attractive young woman should fall for an overweight older man seems an act of wish-fulfilment by an ageing male writer on behalf of an older male audience (Yeates, 1997). It's certainly true that the older man/younger woman relationship is a recurring feature of film and television narratives to a degree that the reverse situation (older woman/younger man) is not. For most viewers, however, it seems entirely within the series' narrative logic. Fitz's intelligence and his heart are Judith's explanation for why 'I've loved you for twenty-five years, and I have never wanted anyone else', as she tells him in 'Lemming'. For Penhaligon, Fitz represents not just the intelligence, wit, bravado and compassionate masculinity that her colleagues lack, but a substitute for the father she has lost. In this respect, however, Fitz proves as deficient as he is with his own family, to whom he returns just as his lover needs him most, in the aftermath of her rape.

To Judith, Penhaligon comes to embody not just a sexual rival but the competition for her husband's attention presented by his police work – which helps to explain one of the series' most shocking lines, when she tells Penhaligon (in 'Brotherly Love'), 'I never thought I'd hear myself say this, but there's a certain poetic justice to it isn't there? To your rape, I mean.' Judith's feminism, in the end, is no match for her envy and rage. To paraphrase Fitz, what she *really* feels overrides what she's *supposed* to feel.

A further reason for Judith's outburst might be the intensified emotion of late pregnancy. The arrival of a third Fitzgerald child signals a new turn in Fitz's domestic life, and provides a background to the tortured family stories of the remainder of *Cracker*'s third and final series. But the birth also serves a symbolic purpose beyond the narrative, as Jimmy McGovern bows out of the series, to be replaced by Paul Abbott. In this context, the child comes to represent McGovern's bequest, his 'handing over the baby' to the younger writer. Accepting the honour, Abbott christens the hitherto unnamed infant Jimmy, perhaps for Fitz's hero Cagney (certainly not for Jimmy Beck), but surely as much for his predecessor in the writer's chair.[15]

Like McGovern, Abbott grew up in a large working-class family in the Northwest – in Burnley, as the ninth of ten children. Both writers knew poverty, but while the bulging McGovern household could be boisterous, the Abbotts' was truly chaotic. Paul's mother left home when he was nine, leaving the children in the 'care' of their alcoholic father, who departed two years later. Thereafter the children were left to fend for themselves, under the guidance of Paul's eldest sister, then seventeen and pregnant. They received child allowance, but otherwise they spurned benefits and supported themselves with whatever jobs they could get, fearful that alerting social services to their situation would mean their dispersal to different local authority homes. Abbott insists that a synopsis of his childhood makes it sound bleaker than it felt at the time, and he has drawn heavily on his experiences in his exuberantly comic drama *Shameless*. Nevertheless, the life took its toll: he was raped by a stranger at eleven, and at fifteen a period of deep depression culminated in a breakdown, a suicide attempt and a spell in a psychiatric ward (Franks, 2002). Hospitalisation was the turning point for Abbott; instead of returning home to his family, he found himself foster parents, with whom he enjoyed 'a more organised period of my life, with my own bed space, clean sheets – like moving into Buckingham Palace' (Brown, 1997). He devoted himself increasingly to writing, having stories published in the likes of *Titbits* and the *Weekly News*. He won a place at Manchester University, where he studied psychology, but left after two years when his first radio play, with an endorsement that Abbott had pestered from Alan Bennett, was broadcast on BBC Radio 4 (in 1982, the same year that McGovern signed up for *Brookside*). Two years later, Abbott would be on the staff of the venerable *Coronation Street*, initially as a story editor, graduating to writing episodes by 1989.

A young man weaves hurriedly between the huge machines on a textile factory shop floor; a pack of women give frantic chase. Amid shrieks of laughter, they force the startled youth to the floor and, ignoring his struggles, begin to remove his trousers and underwear. Not, as it might sound to those familiar with the series, a scene from *Clocking Off* (BBC, 2000–6),[16] the drama that established Abbott as the hottest young writer in British television, but the opening scene of 'Best Boys', his first story for *Cracker*, after his spell as producer on series two. It's a scene typical of Abbott – raucous, exuberant and celebratory of working-class sexuality. 'Best Boys' marks a change of pace and tone, as the incoming writer seeks to leave his own stamp on a series that has until now been indelibly Jimmy McGovern's.

Superficially, the scenario of 'Best Boys' – embittered man meets impetuous, hot-tempered, troubled youth, and together they embark on a killing spree – suggests a reworking of McGovern's 'To Say I Love You', replacing the heterosexual young couple of that story with an older man, Grady (Liam Cunningham) and a seventeen-year-old boy (John Simm). Abbott even appears to acknowledge the parallel by having Fitz assume at first that the killers are a man and a woman. But the writer explicitly distances his story from McGovern's when Fitz briefs the police, 'we're not looking at Bonnie and Clyde'. And while Abbott's first story has to tie up some loose ends, it is also very evidently the work of a different writer, with his own concerns.

The most obvious loose end is the passing of Jimmy Beck. His ghost lingers through much of 'Best Boys', beginning with his funeral ('I wanted to see him burn,' says Penhaligon, 'I was disappointed when I heard it was a burial'). At one point, Jimmy's spirit seems almost to 'possess' another officer, DC Temple (Robert Cavanah), who makes an investigative error reminiscent of Beck's with Albie, and then cravenly attempts to pass the mistake off as PC Skelton's, on the grounds that Skelton 'can afford a mistake; I can't'. When Penhaligon confronts him, Temple wrongfoots her by quoting from Beck's diary, retrieved from the dead man's flat. This spooky scene – Beck's words emerging from Temple's lips – raises the prospect that Penhaligon's erstwhile nemesis will continue to reach out from beyond the grave to hurt and undermine her.

But this narrative arc is left incomplete. Temple may have erred, but his error has less obviously fatal consequences than Beck's, and he is self-evidently a more conscientious policeman, and a more sympathetic character. Rather than employ Beck's diary as a weapon

121

against Penhaligon, he hands it over to her. And while we might expect her to use its contents to vindicate her charge against Beck, Penhaligon chooses instead to destroy the diary, conscious presumably that her ambitions for promotion will fare better if she lets the matter lie. What is, on one level, a ritual of purification or exorcism – Penhaligon purging herself of Beck's memory – is on another the act of one writer stepping out from the shadow of another. It is, in a sense, McGovern's script that Penhaligon feeds into the shredder alongside the pages from Beck's diary. Penhaligon never speaks directly of Beck again, and the prospect of further revelation held out by Fitz's meeting with Beck's sister at the funeral is never followed up, thus freeing up narrative space for Abbott's own purposes.

Gub Neal has suggested that Abbott's arrival ushers in a 'more domestic Fitz' (Neal, 2007). Certainly, McGovern's Fitz never had to take his infant son to work, as he does in 'Best Boys', when he incongruously bottlefeeds him at a crime scene. 'You were supposed to be the little miracle that saved our marriage,' he jokes to little Jimmy in 'True Romance' during another of his arguments with Judith over money. The same story sees Fitz attempting a new understanding with Mark, as a prelude to the kidnap that will be the series climax. In an interrogation scene that is, if not perhaps one of *Cracker*'s very best, then certainly among its most emotionally charged, a desperate Fitz tells Janice, 'Right now I'd die for him. I'd die for my family.'

This line gives a clue to one of the most striking features of the Abbott *Cracker*, its sense of emotional *excess*. While McGovern brought to the series an understanding of drama honed during his *Brookside* years, his stories don't, for the most part, stray too far from the constraints of television realism that bind most British crime drama. Abbott's, however, seem to be straining for an altogether more hyperbolic melodramatic mode, one more familiar from American daytime soaps than from their more grounded British cousins: they are more *The Bold and the Beautiful* than *Brookside*. Fitz's response to the news of Mark's kidnap is a case in point. 'No! Oh God, no! No, please,

Sexual predators: Janice

... and *Black Narcissus*'s Sister Ruth

123

God!' he cries as he reads Janice's fax, lifting his left hand to his forehead: dialogue and performance unite in an almost parodic re-enactment of 'cheap' melodrama. When Janice prepares herself for her moment of confrontation with Fitz, meanwhile, the camera frames her lower face in close-up as she applies her lurid red lipstick, in homage to a celebrated shot embodying the sexually and homicidally predatory character of Kathleen Byron's demented nun Sister Ruth in Powell and Pressburger's *Black Narcissus* (1947) – a film and partnership both once derided for vulgar excess.

This employment of a critically unfavoured generic mode continues in still more knowing fashion during Fitz's interrogation of Janice. 'A few months ago,' Fitz explains, 'Mark got his girlfriend pregnant – Debbie was her name – and he's depressed because she lost the baby, and he's depressed because she gave him the big kiss-off.' Not only does this *feel* like an American soap 'catch-up' ('previously on *Cracker*'), but the sensation of unreality is heightened when we cut away from Fitz and Janice to Judith, captivated by their exchange on CCTV, exactly as if she were a stereotypically soap-addicted housewife. 'True Romance', we should note, is a convincing title for a daytime US soap.

Judith, though, is not the only audience in the narrative. Earlier, as Fitz makes a televised appeal to her to release Mark, Janice watches, tears streaming down her face, and exclaims, 'look what they've done to you'. Janice, we learn, has for months or even years been hooked on the soap opera of Fitz's life, tracing the rising and falling contours of his marriage and his relationship with Penhaligon. Like the heroine of the later *Nurse Betty* (2000), who retreats into the world of her favourite daytime medical soap after the trauma of witnessing her drug-dealing husband's murder, Janice is pathologically immersed, possessed by the perverse delusion that she merits a real part in the life of her fantasy object, Fitz. Janice's dissociation ('look what *they've* done to you') emphasises her distorted sense of reality: but where Betty's fantasy is ultimately benevolent, Janice is a deranged fan in the mould of Sandra Bernhard's Masha in Martin Scorsese's *King of Comedy* (1981), Kathy Bates's Annie in *Misery* (1990) or, especially, Jessica Walter's Evelyn in Clint Eastwood's *Play Misty for Me* (1971), in which Evelyn's target, Dave Garver (Eastwood), is, like Fitz (in one of his roles), a radio DJ. Like Evelyn, whose repeated requests give Eastwood's film its title, Janice has a favourite song, Dusty Springfield's 'I Close My Eyes and Count to Ten', which she plays to drown out her victims' screams. The overwrought ballad not only fits the emotional pitch of the story, its lyrics further reinforce Janice's problems in distinguishing between reality and her fantasies ('It's a feeling so unreal/Somehow I can't believe it's true').

124

Engrossed viewers:
Janice

. . . and Judith

Life as TV soap

Janice's delusional personality and her fixation on Fitz are explained by her sense of loss for the father who, in her eyes, didn't love her enough to sexually abuse her as he did her two sisters. Seventeen-year-old Bill Preece/Nash in Abbott's previous story, 'Best Boys', is another fantasist with parental issues. An orphan, he was fostered at seven and was on the brink of adoption when his foster mother unexpectedly became pregnant, condemning him to a childhood in local authority care and a festering bitterness at his rejection. It is this vulnerability in Bill that awakens a protective instinct in Grady, foreman of the textile factory where Bill works, who reluctantly gives Bill a place to stay. When Grady's landlady (Jackie Downey) discovers a shirtless Bill the following morning, she takes him for a prostitute and threatens Grady with eviction, a threat that provokes Bill's impetuous temper and brings about her own death.

Mrs Franklin's snap judgment – that Grady and Bill are a homosexual couple – thereafter becomes the dominant interpretation of their relationship. 'Why's a bloke that age wanna be your friend?', asks Bill's social worker, McVerry (Paul Barber). Once again, the assumption precedes the accuser's murder; as with Mrs Franklin, what is initiated by Bill is completed with brutal efficiency by Grady, a trained soldier discharged for 'inconsistent behaviour'. This *modus operandi* leads Fitz to conclude first that the killers are a man and a woman and, later, an older and younger man. But he quickly discards an initial hypothesis that the killers are father and son, convinced instead that this is a new gay relationship.

But is it? The text certainly offers evidence to support this interpretation. After the second murder, Grady wakes up in his car having fallen asleep on Bill's shoulder. Immediately after Fitz outlines his theory while feeding baby Jimmy, we cut to an extreme long-shot of Bill washing his shirt in a canal while Grady, in the foreground, gazes at his half-naked body. Grady, when he is finally captured and interrogated, never denies desiring the younger man, insisting only that 'nothing happened'. 'That's the waste,' laments Fitz, 'Bill Nash offered you the best ever chance of making all this mean something.' But if Bill is certainly seeking love, there's no suggestion he's seeking sex. While he may be sexualised by Grady's gaze (and by Dick Dodd's camera, which is repeatedly drawn to his hairless chest), Bill is an entirely passive object of erotic fascination both to the older man and the women in the factory. Even the cola he drinks stresses his innocence: not Coke or Pepsi, but *Virgin*. As Fitz tells Grady, 'Bill Nash is still very much a child,' and the child in Bill brings out the father in Grady.

When Grady is visited by DC Temple, Bill assumes the role of Grady's son, looking for his misplaced trainers. Later, in a shopping

Grady and Bill: as lovers

127

. . . and as father and son

centre, Grady presents Bill with a new pair of trainers, as if symbolically accepting the part he has been offered. When McVerry questions Grady's motives, Bill replies 'I picked him. What's wrong with that?' Far from the admission of a sexual relationship that McVerry takes this to be, this is in fact a defiant statement of self-determination. Until now, social workers like McVerry have made all the decisions concerning Bill's welfare and upbringing; in the wake of their failure, Bill is seizing that right for himself, 'picking' his own family. While he relentlessly pursues the Nashes (in a campaign of harassment that has been going on for years), he focuses his longing on his one-time mother, Diane (Annette Ekblom), and turns his hatred and bitterness on her husband (Dominic Rigby). Finally, desperate at his separation from Grady, Bill attempts to build a family by force. Capturing Diane and her youngest son, Steven (Anthony Lewis), and holding them at gunpoint (at an archetypal 'family event', a funfair), Bill demands the presence of the one person he needs to complete his fantasy family: Grady.

'White Ghost', broadcast as a feature-length 'one-off' nearly a year after 'True Romance', introduces another survivor from a damaged family. An Essex-born small businessman out of his depth in Britain's last dependent colony, Dennis Philby (Barnaby Kay) is, in the story's resonant acronym, 'FILTH: Failed In London, Try Hong Kong'. Up to his ears in debt, Dennis takes revenge on the one-time friend (Benedict Wong) who exploits his misfortune for his own business gain. But although the death of Peter Yang buys Dennis time to save his business, it is not, at root, financially motivated. Dennis is driven to murder by the threat to his dreams of family when his Chinese girlfriend, Su Lin (Liu Jo Ying), threatens to abort their unborn child; his second victim is the abortionist Su Lin has already consulted. To prevent Su Lin carrying out her threat by other means, Dennis imprisons her in a shipping container, where he marries her in a ludicrous sham ceremony. The baby has talismanic significance to Dennis, who, like Bill Nash, is of uncertain parentage. He is, we learn, the child of his mother's adulterous affair; his fear of the dark stems from the hours that he spent locked in a darkened garage during his mother's illicit liaisons – a humiliation he revisits on the unfortunate Su Lin. Dennis plans to avenge his mother's betrayal by returning to England to present the baby to the husband she wronged, the man he still considers his father.

'White Ghost' was not well received. Critics who had praised Abbott's first two stories now felt that the character and the concept had passed their sell-by date, 'Lost in Honkers' as the *Guardian*'s review put it. The bigger budget and expansive action (including at one point, a helicopter pursuit) may have been part of the problem. Performance and production, driven presumably by a desire to capture an international audience, uneasily mimicked the brushed-steel sheen of high-budget US TV drama, with the 'exotic' Hong Kong setting only reinforcing the sense of an updated *Hawaii Five-O* (CBS, 1968–80). In the process, the story jettisoned too many of the elements that had made *Cracker* special – the familiar and grounding landscape of Manchester, the sense of interiority, of lives like our own blown off course. Of Fitz's habitual foils, only Wise was retained, but the previously combative DCI was largely reduced to the status of bumbling sidekick, an ersatz Dr Watson. Most of all it missed Judith and Penhaligon, the counterweights to Fitz's otherwise improbable genius. Without them our hero seemed to flounder, a Fitz out of water.

6 Life after Death

In November 1996, just weeks after the lukewarm reviews for 'White Ghost', Granada announced a new deal with ABC that would bring *Cracker* to US screens. This was not a distribution deal – the original series had already screened on the cable channel Arts & Entertainment (A & E) Network, to strong reviews and a modest but dedicated audience – but a partnership, from which would come a new, American *Cracker*.

While game-show and comedy formats regularly cross the Atlantic in both directions, selling a drama format was a first for Granada, and enthusiasm was high. Gub Neal was to be executive producer, working alongside independent production company Kushner-Locke, to keep Granada's interests represented and to maintain some creative link with the original series. Twenty-six episodes were planned for the first run – with some stories adapted from the original scripts (ultimately four of McGovern's, two of Abbott's, plus one new Abbott story) and others contributed by American writers. There was talk of how the series might develop over five years or more. The run began on 18 September 1997, almost exactly four years after *Cracker*'s first UK outing. But despite reasonably favourable early reviews, the show failed to find its audience – those who'd seen the original were hostile, others were unenthusiastic – and ABC dropped it after episode eleven (the five remaining completed episodes were later screened on A & E).

Neal would have better luck some years later with *Queer as Folk* (Channel 4, 1999–2000), but the *Cracker* venture, he believes, was cursed before it began. Casting Fitz was always going to be challenging, but in the New Jersey-born James Gandolfini he thought he had found an actor 'as close as you could have got to Fitz'. The future *Sopranos* (HBO, 1999–2007) star was tempted, but felt unable to compete with Coltrane's performance. In the end, Coltrane's shoes were filled by Robert Pastorelli, another bulky actor from New Jersey, best known from the CBS sitcom *Murphy Brown* (1988–98). By the time of shooting, though, Pastorelli had given up smoking, and lost three stone. Worse, it was proving harder than Neal had hoped to preserve the essence of the original:

> The network had come down and said 'well of course we won't sell it in Salt Lake if there's any drinking, swearing or smoking in it' . . . You could see the plastic wrapping just beginning to get sucked in around it. (Neal, 2007)

It's easy to dismiss the US *Cracker* – the smoothing down of Fitz's rougher edges (and, this being LA, naturally he has to drive); the way he is forever playing with a cigarette, but never seems to *light* it; the wooden Josh Hartnett, here in his first screen role as Fitz's not-quite-so-wayward son (rechristened Michael); the discarding of McGovern's more astringent religious commentary (which *definitely* wouldn't sell in Salt Lake) and most of his critique of the police. The inexperienced, out-of-his-depth Bilborough is replaced by the mature, close-to-retirement, grouchy but fair Lieutenant Fry (R. Lee Ermey), who, unlike his English counterpart, manages to leave the force in one piece. Beck becomes the altogether more palatable Detective Danny Watlington (Robert Wisdom), black not Irish and with his prejudices (though not, interestingly, his homophobia) a lot more contained. And the affair between Fitz and his Penhaligon – now a blonde, Detective Hannah Tyler (Angela Featherstone) – fails to convince, partly because she is so much more self-assured than our Panhandle.

Heavier on the melodrama from the start, the series kicks off not with McGovern's 'Mad Woman' but Abbott's 'True Romance' – whose family-in-peril storyline, it was felt, stood the best chance of

America's Fitz – with unlit cigarette

gripping a new audience. But the series is not without its rewards.
Pastorelli is never permitted to reach the depths of despair and self-
destruction we expect of Fitz, but he brings to the character a louche,
dishevelled arrogance that might have won us over were it not for
Coltrane's memory (although in truth Pastorelli's performance recalls
Elliott Gould's hangdog Philip Marlowe in Robert Altman's 1974 *The
Long Goodbye* more than it does Coltrane's Fitz). It's not completely
craven: McGovern's confrontational soliloquy from 'Mad Woman' is
largely preserved, and in place of Albie and his Hillsborough rage the US
version intriguingly gives us a Latino sniper targeting black women in
revenge for the random, near-fatal assault on his wife during the 1992
LA riots. Overall, though, the series feels rudderless, and despite Paul
Abbott's late attempt at a salvage operation with the penultimate two-
parter, 'First Love' (one of the stories not shown by ABC) – a new story
in which he killed off the Penhaligon character and introduced a new

Lieutenant with a striking resemblance to Christopher Eccleston's Bilborough – the guest appearance from Robbie Coltrane in the final story, 'Faustian Fitz', as a paedophilic Hollywood producer, only highlighted its deficiencies (though for a more generous assessment, see Page, 2000).

Regardless of its independent strengths or weaknesses, the American *Cracker* was, for those mourning the absence of the 'real' Fitz, a poor substitute (the US series was shown in the UK in a graveyard slot, to be largely ignored by critics and viewers). Both McGovern and Coltrane had let it be known that they might consider a return for Fitz if either one came up with a strong enough story (implicitly Coltrane seemed to rule out a collaboration with any other writer). Both, however, were kept occupied with other projects.

Meanwhile, fictional representations of forensic psychologists proliferated in film – *Kiss the Girls* (1997) and its sequel *Along Came a Spider* (2001), *The Bone Collector* (1999), the continuing Hannibal Lecter franchise (*Hannibal*, 2001; *Red Dragon*, 2002) – and on television – *Halifax p.f.* (Channel 9, Australia, 1994–2001), *Millennium* (Fox, 1996–9), *Profiler* (NBC, 1996–2000), *Waking the Dead*, *Wire in the Blood* (ITV, 2002–), *Criminal Minds* (CBS, 2005–). Lynda La Plante's *Mind Games* (ITV, 2001), was a direct challenge to *Cracker*. Its detective-cum-profiler heroine, DI Frances O'Neil (Fiona Shaw), is an Irish-born former nun (unlike Fitz, she retains her faith) who rubs up against more traditionalist colleagues suspicious of her methods. Her mockers make disparaging remarks at the expense of her former occupation, dubbing her 'Mother Teresa' and, tellingly, 'nun on the run' (the 1990 film *Nuns on the Run* starred Robbie Coltrane). 133

Several other recent screen heroes, while not sharing Fitz's occupation, are recognisably similar in their approaches. The police heroine (Kyra Sedgwick) of *The Closer* (TNT, 2005–), uses psychological insights and strategies to 'crack' suspects in cases where more instinct-driven detective skills prove inadequate; the series is also structurally similar to *Cracker* in its privileging of the dynamics of interrogation over investigative enigma. Paul Abbott's post-*Cracker* effort *Touching Evil* (ITV, 1997–9) has a similarly intuitive hero, and a (female) criminal psychologist in a supporting role.

In late 2005, news filtered out that *Cracker* was to return, with McGovern and Coltrane in place. There were even rumours that the one-off would lead to a new series. Finally, in October 2006 – ten years to the month after 'White Ghost' – the speculation came to an end.

Even those who hadn't learned months in advance – in the excited chatter of internet fansites and bulletin boards that had been barely dreamt of when the series was at its height – could deduce something of the theme of 'Cracker' from the hyperactive title montage, in which images of Manchester's rebuilding collide with news footage of the Twin Towers attack and the conflicts in Iraq, Afghanistan and Northern Ireland, all accompanied by frenetic breakbeat music, news reports and bellicose speeches from George Bush and Tony Blair. This reflection of a media-saturated, *News 24* age is not limited to the title sequence. Images and sounds of the ongoing 'war on terror' are ubiquitous: televisions and radios relay a ceaseless index of chaos and mounting casualties. This, as Robbie Coltrane told Melvyn Bragg in a *South Bank Show* profile timed to coincide with the drama, was the subject that had inspired in McGovern the 'fine and just anger' necessary to revive his most famous creation. Director Antonia Bird (who last worked with McGovern on *Priest*), gave the drama an accentuated stylistic sheen, and picked up the pace to suit a post-*24* (Fox Network, 2001–), post-*Spooks* (BBC, 2002–) TV thriller world.

Meanwhile, changed landscapes – personal, physical, political – dominate the narrative. Where Abbott's 'White Ghost' left Fitz in Hong Kong, McGovern retrieves him from even further afield, explaining his long absence as a seven-year relocation to Australia ('home of skin cancer and Skippy,' he sneers). Fitz's return – for Katie's (Stefanie Willmore) wedding – shows us through his eyes a new, alien Manchester, the city centre comprehensively rebuilt after the IRA's 1996 bomb. Much has changed in Fitz's life, too. He and Judith are now in late middle-age – greyer, more lined – and grandparents. Mark has somehow acquired a wife (Rosina Carbone) and a young daughter (Lilla-Ella Kelleher), and membership of the property-owning classes.

All the same, the opening scenes work to reassure us that we are still dealing with the same indefatigable Fitz. At the wedding he antagonises the groom's father with his provocative analysis of 9/11 ('Didn't you say to yourself, "Hang on, hang on, Twin Towers first, then the Pentagon, then plane out of the sky? Where's your sense of dramatic structure?"'), before a rambling, drunken speech that insults the groom and upsets the bride. Elsewhere, he neglects his family in favour of 'caped crusader nonsense', uses blackmail methods to draw out a reluctant witness, and routinely ignores the 'no smoking' notices scattered around the steel-and-glass colossus that is the Greater Manchester Police Force's new headquarters. There is even a trip to the casino, albeit with Judith in tow and holding tight to the purse strings.

Fitz's quarry is Kenny Archer (Anthony Flanagan), a former soldier, now a policeman tormented by flashbacks of his tours in Northern Ireland and the conviction that, as he tells a Samaritans volunteer, 'if I don't kill myself, I'll kill others'. His first victim is an

135

Haunted by Northern Ireland: Kenny

American comedian who enrages Kenny with a routine in which he disparagingly compares the IRA with Al-Qaida ('you call that terrorism?') and sardonically celebrates American military force while offering thanks to Britain for road-testing dubious antiterrorist strategies – 'dawn raids, internment, torture, shoot-to-kill'. American arrogance, it transpires, is Kenny's bugbear: in his eyes, the British army toured Northern Ireland 'with one arm behind our back'. By contrast, 'as soon as a few Americans get hit . . . [they] destroy everything. Men, women, children . . .'. Kenny holds Americans responsible for the IRA attacks that killed his friends. As he tells his second victim, 'I want revenge for every British soldier killed in Northern Ireland', revenge for 'every bullet that hit every British soldier bought with American dollars. Every bomb, bought with American dollars.' As Fitz realises – perhaps a little too readily – Kenny's problem is that 9/11 has seen the conflict in Northern Ireland rendered trivial in the eyes of media and politicians, emptying of meaning both his own traumas and the sacrifice of his friends and colleagues:

'It wasn't a war,' that's what they're saying now, 'Compared to 9/11, Afghanistan, Iraq, Northern Ireland was just a bunfight. So stop being naughty boys, kiss and make up, 'cause we've got far more important things to do nowadays.' Totally insignificant: so what did your mates die for?

While the political insight was new and striking, other elements invoked the ghost of *Cracker* past. Kenny is a clear descendant of Albie, a killer rationalising his acts in terms of a spurious 'mission' of revenge; but he also resembles Jimmy Beck – another Samaritans-calling policeman driven to the edge by guilt and grief at the death of a close colleague. Elsewhere, we are introduced to a hotheaded, overconfident senior investigating officer, who fondly anticipates media glory but recoils from the implications of Fitz's conclusions (Richard Coyle's DI Walters: three parts Bilborough, one part Wise); a detective suckered by a false story of incapacity into releasing a key suspect; and a young female officer who attracts Judith's resentment. Consciously or otherwise, McGovern even recycles an old *Cracker* name – although there's no obvious resemblance

Troubled cops:
Beck

... and Kenny

137

between the bereaved mother Jean Molloy (Lisa Eichhorn) and the simple-minded sex offender from 'One Day a Lemming Will Fly'. Such allusions make for an entertaining game of nostalgia for the established fan, but undermine any impression of a drama looking forwards.

There were, though, rewards: a scene between Fitz and Judith while he searches the internet for chemical cures for his impotence (he blames the passing of youth, she, more realistically, cites 'whisky in profusion and cigarettes in abundance'), is affectingly tender, while Anthony Flanagan's complex performance shows the bubbling anger and torment beneath Kenny's surface calm more effectively than the overused flashbacks.

It wasn't quite the critical triumph that ITV had hoped for: reviews judged the new story below par for *Cracker*, and expressed disappointment at the perceived 'anti-Americanism', though most still thought it better than the genre average. But executives had cause to celebrate the ratings. At 8.2 million, it comfortably beat the old enemy, *Casualty*, and its spin-off, *Holby City* (BBC, 1999–), as well as *Spooks* and the inferior *Cracker* imitator, *Wire in the Blood*. *Prime Suspect*, revived for a seventh and final outing a fortnight later, could manage only 7.2 million (though the critics, with some justice, rated Jane Tennison's return more satisfying than Fitz's). Still, it wasn't, perhaps, the epitaph that the series deserved.

Will Fitz be back? Coltrane hasn't ruled it out, but McGovern is doubtful, stung less by the criticism of the last special than by his own conviction that the exercise was a mistake from the start. Though born in the 90s, Fitz was, he says, a product of the 80s, and certainly out of step with the Britain of the smoking ban (McGovern, 2007a). And McGovern has other stories to tell. *The Street*, the 2006 series of interlocking single dramas (building on a form established by *Boys from the Blackstuff* and revived in Paul Abbott's *Clocking Off*) which he co-wrote and oversaw for BBC1, was a surprise (for some) BAFTA best drama series winner, beating the favourite, the clever but frothy *Life on Mars* (BBC, 2006–7); at the time of writing, a third series is on the way.

In any case, another return for Fitz might be stretching credibility a step too far. Gub Neal notes that the unavoidable outcome of that ceaselessly self-destructive lifestyle would be an early grave (Neal, 2007), a point that McGovern, himself rather calmer these days (and an ex-smoker) concedes. (McGovern, 2007b). The 2006 'Cracker' even teases us with the possibility that Fitz might have been shot by Kenny, just before the killer meets his own death from a police sniper's bullet. Realistically, the return of *Cracker* would have to be dominated by the series' fourth funeral – that of Fitz himself. In his absence, we're free perhaps to imagine the kind of peaceful, contented retirement – finally, more 'Fitz and Judith on the straight and narrow' than 'Bogart and Hepburn on the *African Queen*' – that McGovern, at least, is unlikely ever to write for him.

Notes

1 The *Sun* was not the only newspaper to publish such stories, but it was the most wholehearted. The stories were complete fabrications, and had largely come from anonymous police sources, including the Police Federation and senior South Yorkshire officers (Scraton, 2000). Sales of the paper on Merseyside plummeted overnight, and never completely recovered (see also Chippendale and Horrie, 1992).

2 When the American *Cracker* made its way back over the Atlantic, it appeared in the ITV schedules as *Fitz*, to avoid confusion with the UK version.

3 The city has even given its name to a particularly brutal act of violence: the 'Glasgow kiss', or head butt, which Fitz memorably delivers to Jimmy Beck in 'Brotherly Love'.

4 In American slang, 'to panhandle' is to beg on the streets; Fitz's epithet for Penhaligon thus emphasises and arguably reinforces her lowly status.

5 The exception is 'Brotherly Love', in which, although we see the first murder by David Harvey, the story keeps us guessing who is responsible for the two that follow – calling into question, at least for the police, the guilt of their original suspect, who was in custody at the time of the two later murders.

6 The theme of the man (or, occasionally, woman) falsely accused was one of Hitchcock's favourites, emerging as early as *The Lodger* (1926), his second film as director. The theme was developed in later films, notably *Blackmail* (1929), *The 39 Steps* (1935), *Young and Innocent* (1937), *Spellbound* (1945), *I Confess* (1953),

The Wrong Man (1956) and *North by Northwest* (1959). McGovern, though, cites as inspiration the American TV series *The Fugitive* (ABC, 1963–7), the saga of Dr Richard Kimble's (David Janssen) quest to prove himself innocent of murdering his wife (Crace, 1995).

7 Mo's promotion in *Between the Lines* is shortlived – she is soon dismissed on disciplinary grounds, although there's no suggestion that either her gender or her sexuality is a factor. Penhaligon's ascent occurs in the interim between the end of series three and the special *White Ghost*, when DCI Wise appears in Hong Kong in her place, much to Fitz's (and many fans') disappointment.

8 The rape conviction rate has since fallen further, to below 6 per cent in 2007.

9 *Brazil* and 'To Be a Somebody' both display a thematic preoccupation with culpability, revenge and explosions, while their protagonists also exhibit delusions of motive (behind Gilliam's Sam Lowry's (Jonathan Pryce) quest for justice for the mistaken execution of Mr Buttle is his desire for Buttle's neighbour, Jill (Kim Griest)). Just as *Brazil*'s Sam escapes from grim reality into his vivid fantasy world, Albie retreats under stress into his football chants and evocations of Liverpool football triumphs; both characters finally withdraw completely into their own respective worlds. Further echoes of *Brazil* can be seen in the recurring comic interludes involving the 'cowboy' plumbers who wreck Fitz's bathroom, much as the two engineers (played by Bob Hoskins and Derrick O'Connor) wreak havoc in Sam Lowry's apartment.

139

10 At a private screening of 'To Be a Somebody' that McGovern organised for the Hillsborough Families Support Group, Bilborough's death was initially greeted with scepticism. McGovern recalls hearing Trevor Hicks, then the group's chairman (who was, ironically, later portrayed by Christopher Eccleston in McGovern's dramadoc, *Hillsborough*), say to his ex-wife as the credits rolled, 'I bet he's alive in part three.' In the end, though, the families, says McGovern 'loved that notion of killing the *Sun* reporter, the copper'; several admitted that in their grief they had fantasised about doing the same thing (McGovern, 2007a).

11 Fitz's idea is presumably inspired by *EastEnders*' Leslie Grantham, who served ten years of a life sentence for murder before he was immortalised as 'Dirty Den'. Cynics might wonder if Fitz's proposal would find a welcome on the post-*Big Brother* Channel 4.

12 This sequence was among several in the first episode of 'Brotherly Love' to be edited after first broadcast, which originally ran some ten minutes longer than *Cracker*'s usual sixty-minute slot. With the Penhaligon–Beck cliffhanger to resolve, McGovern and producer Hilary Bevan Jones had persuaded Granada to allow the extra

time, but in the process caused media controversy when it emerged that ITN's *News at Ten* would be delayed as a result. Under pressure from the regulator, ITV was forced to move the offending episode from Monday to Sunday night. The edited version is, to the best of my knowledge, the one that has been used for all subsequent UK and overseas screenings, as well as all VHS and DVD releases. The uncut original episode survives in the BFI's National Archive.

13 Bilborough's plea to 'Jimmy' seems to reach out even beyond the text – to the writer, as well as to Beck.

14 Fitz's role as radio therapist brings him into the territory of *Frasier* (NBC, 1993–2004), TV's most popular psychiatrist. Fitz is also heard on occasion using that character's on-air catchphrase, 'I'm listening', which may or may not be a deliberate allusion to the US sitcom.

15 It was presumably in homage to their former colleague that somebody on the *Brookside* team chose to name Jimmy Corkhill's dog 'Cracker'.

16 The sense of inverted *déja vu* is compounded by the fact that John Simm, who plays the pursued youth, turns up in the opening episode of *Clocking Off*.

Bibliography

Alibhai-Brown, Yasmin, *Mixed Blessings: The Complex Lives of Mixed Race Britons* (London: Women's Press, 2001).

Ariès, Philippe, *Western Attitudes towards Death: From the Middle Ages to the Present* (London: Marion Boyers, 1976).

Britton, Paul, *The Jigsaw Man* (London: Corgi, 2001).

Brown, Maggie, 'The Best Stuff Comes from Real Life', *Daily Telegraph*, 25 April 1997.

Brunsdon, Charlotte, 'Structure of Anxiety: Recent British Television Crime Fiction', *Screen* vol. 39 no. 3, Autumn 1998, pp. 223–43.

Butler, Robert, 'The Man Who Raped Sheila Grant', *Independent on Sunday*, 5 February 1995.

Chippendale, Peter and Horrie, Chris, *Stick It Up Your Punter! The Rise and Fall of The Sun* (London: Mandarin, 1992).

Clarke, Alan, 'This Is Not the Boy Scouts: Television Police Series and Definitions of Law and Order', in Tony Bennett, Colin Mercer and Jane Woollacott (eds), *Popular Culture and Social Relations* (Milton Keynes: Open University Press, 1986).

Collins, Michael, *The Likes of Us: A Biography of the White Working Class* (London: Granta, 2004).

Cook, Stephen, *The Real Cracker: Investigating the Criminal Mind* (London: Channel 4 Books, 2001).

Cooke, Lez, *British Television Drama: A History* (London: BFI, 2003).

Crace, John, *Cracker: The Truth behind the Fiction* (2nd edn) (London: Boxtree, 1995).

Creeber, Glen, 'Old Sleuth or New Man? Investigations in Rape, Murder and Masculinity in *Cracker* (1993–96)', *Continuum: Journal of Media & Cultural Studies* vol. 16 no. 2, 2002, pp. 169–83.

Creeber, Glen, *The Singing Detective* (London: BFI, 2007).

Day-Lewis, Sean, *Talk of Drama* (Luton: University of Luton Press, 1998).

Eaton, Mary, 'A Fair Cop? Viewing the Effects of Canteen Culture in *Prime Suspect* and *Between the Lines*,' in David Kidd-Hewitt and Richard Osborne (eds), *Crime and the Media: The Postmodern Spectacle* (London: Pluto Press, 1995).

Franks, Alan, 'Screenplays from the Edge', *The Times Magazine*, 26 January 2002.

Geraghty, Christine, *Women and Soap Opera* (Cambridge: Polity Press, 1991).

Geraghty, Christine, 'Social Issues and Realist Soaps: A Study of British Soaps in the 1980s/1990s', in Robert C. Allen (ed.), *To Be Continued: Soap Opera around the World* (London/New York: Routledge, 1995).

Gibson, Owen, 'It's Not That Grim up North', *Guardian*, 27 March 2006.

Gledhill, Christine, 'Speculations on the Relationship between Soap Opera and Melodrama', *Quarterly Review of Film and Video* vol. 14 nos 1–2, 1992.

Gorer, Geoffrey, *Death, Grief and Mourning in Contemporary Britain* (London: Cresset Press, 1965).

Gregory, Jeanne and Lees, Sue, *Policing Sexual Assault* (London: Routledge, 1999).

Halford, Alison, *No Way up the Greasy Pole* (London: Constable, 1993).

Jeffries, Stuart , 'Why I Write', *Guardian*, 7 February 2003.

Littlewood, Jane, 'The Denial of Death and Rites of Passage in Contemporary Societies', in David Clark (ed), *The Sociology of Death* (Oxford: Blackwell, 1993).

McGovern, Jimmy, *NME* Interview, 21 October 1995.

McGovern, Jimmy, Interview with the author, 21 June 2007a.

McGovern, Jimmy, Interview with the author, 20 September 2007b.

Meades, Jonathan, *Observer*, 5 October 1997.

Morrison, Blake, 'Life after James', *Guardian*, 6 February 2003.

Neal, Gub, Interview with the author, April 2007.

Page, Adrian, *Cracking Morse Code: Semiotics and Television Drama* (Luton: University of Luton Press, 2000).

Parkes, Colin Murray, 'Psychiatric Problems following Bereavement by Murder or Manslaughter', *British Journal of Psychiatry* no. 162, 1993, pp. 49–54.

Parkes, Colin Murray, *Bereavement: Studies in Grief in Adult Life* (3rd edn) (London: Penguin, 1998).

Pearce, Edward, *The Times*, 23 April 1989.

Potter, Dennis, *Seeing the Blossom: Two Interviews and a Lecture* (London: Faber and Faber, 1984).

Rock, Paul, *After Homicide* (Oxford: Clarendon Press, 1998).

Scraton, Phil, *Hillsborough: The Truth* (2nd edn) (Edinburgh: Mainstream Publishing, 2000).

Stephen, Iain, 'Robbie, Fitz and Me: A Venture into Television', *The Psychologist* vol. 7 no. 1, January 1994.

Taylor, Lord Justice, *Interim Report into the Hillsborough Stadium Disaster* (London: HMSO, 1989).

Taylor, Rogan, *Football and Its Fans* (Leicester: Leicester University Press, 1992).

Walter, Tony, 'The Mourning after Hillsborough', *Sociological Review* no. 39, pp. 599–625.

Westlake, Michael, 'The Classic TV Detective Genre', *Framework* no. 13, Autumn 1980.

Willis, Pauline, 'Bubbles and Squeeks', *Guardian*, 9 April 1986.

Yeates, Helen, 'Cracking the Code: Looking at Men Letting It All Hang Out', *Metro* no. 110, 1997.

Credits

Cracker
United Kingdom/1993–4
United Kingdom/US/1995

directed by
Michael Winterbottom [1]
Andy Wilson [2]
Simon Cellan Jones [3]
Tim Fywell [4, 9]
Julian Jarrold [5]
Jean Stewart [6]
Roy Battersby [7]
Charles McDougall [8]
produced by
Gub Neal [1–3]
Paul Abbott [4–6]
Hilary Bevan Jones [7–9]
executive producers
Sally Head [1–7, 9]
Gub Neal [8]
For A & E Network:
Delia Fine [7–9]
written by
Jimmy McGovern [1–4, 6, 7]
Ted Whitehead [5]
Paul Abbott [8, 9]
directors of photography
Ivan Strasberg [1–6]
Dick Dodd [7–9]
production designers
Chris Wilkinson [1–3]
Stephen Fineren [4, 6–9]
Claire Kenny [5]
film editors
Trevor Waite [1]
Oral Norrie Ottey [2, 5]
Chris Gill [3]
Edward Mansell [4, 7]
Tony Cranstoun [6, 8]
Anthony Ham [9]
music composed and
performed by
Julian Wastall [1]
Roger Jackson [2, 3]
David Ferguson [4–6]
Rick Wentworth [7–9]

© Granada Television
production company
a Granada Television
production
in association with A & E
Network [7–9]

production executive
Craig McNeil [2–9]
production manager
Liam Foster [1–3]
Des Hughes [4–9]
production supervisor
Bill Leather [4–9]
production co-ordinator
Tracy Lee [1–3, 8, 9]
Eileen Wood [4–6]
location manager
Ken Mair [1–7, 9]
Sue de Beauvoir [8]
assistant directors
1st: John Friend Newman [1, 5]
1st: Peter Shaw [2, 4, 6–8]
1st: Emma Bodger [3]
1st: Vinny Fahy [9]
2nd: Emma Bodger [1, 2]
2nd: Rachel Longhurst [3]
2nd: Jude Harrison [4–9]
2nd unit director
Gareth Milne [7]
continuity
Dorothy Friend [1–6]
Sue Wild [7–9]
casting
Gail Stevens [1–6]
Andy Prior [4–6]
Marilyn Johnson [7, 9]
Andrew Hall [8]
David Shaw [9]
script editor
Catriona McKenzie [1–3]
Nicola Shindler [1–3]
Debbie Shewell [4, 6]
Roxy Spencer [4, 6]
Patrick Spence [7, 9]
script associate
Gwenda Bagshaw [1–7, 9]
Catriona McKenzie [8]

camera operator
Mike Miller [7–9]
focus puller
Richard Brierley [1–9]
grips
Mike Fisher [1, 7–9]
Bob Gregory [2–6]
Peter Maghie [4–6]
Gary Stanton [7–9]
steadicam
Simon Bray [1]
Peter Robinson [2]
Alf Tramontin [2, 4, 5]
Howard Smith [6]
assistant film editor
Chris Clarkson [6, 9]
David Boyle [9]
graphic designer
Phil Buckley [1–9]
art director
Deborah Morley [1–3]
Dave Butterworth [4]
Chris Coldwell [5]
Nick Wilkinson [6]
Bill Crutcher [7–9]
Mark Stonehouse [9]
assistant designer
Rod Gorwood [7, 9]
visual effects
Steve Tomkow
prop buyer
Ron Pritchard [1–9]
prop master
Nigel Place [7, 9]
costume designer
Janty Yates [1–3]
Jean Kelly [4–6]
Tudor George [7–9]
wardrobe supervisor
Sally Mason [1–2]
Michael Richards [7–9]
make-up supervisor
Helen King [1–5]
Sue Milton [7, 9]
Anastasia Shirley [8]
summertime and stormy
weather sung by
Carol Kidd [1]

sound mixer
Phil Smith [1–9]
dubbing editor
John Rutherford [1, 4–6]
John Thomas [1]
Philip Bothamley [2]
Tim Vine [2]
John Crumpton [2]
Max Hoskins [3]
John Senior [4–9]
Chris Clarkson [5]
Mark Briscoe [7–9]
dubbing mixer
John Whitworth [1–3, 5–9]
Andy Wyatt [3, 4]
stunt co-ordinator
Peter Brayham [1, 2, 4, 6]
Chris Webb [1, 7]
Dave Holland [3]
Andy Bradford [6]
forensic psychology consultant
Ian B. Stephen [7]

series one
regular cast
Robbie Coltrane
Fitz
Geraldine Somerville
DS Penhaligon
Barbara Flynn
Judith Fitzgerald
Lorcan Cranitch
DS Beck
Christopher Eccleston
DCI Bilborough
Kieran O'Brien
Mark Fitzgerald
Tess Thomson
Katie Fitzgerald
Edward Peel
Chief Superintendent

1 the mad woman in the attic
After a female student is
brutally murdered on a train,
all the evidence points to a
man found covered in blood
near the line. The suspect,
however, claims amnesia. At
the behest of her parents, the
girl's former tutor, psychologist
Dr Fitzgerald ('Fitz'), offers his
professional help, but is
removed from the case by the
senior officer, DCI Bilborough,

after he suggests that the
suspect, Kelly, is innocent.
With the help of the
undervalued DS Jane
Penhaligon, Fitz manages to
restore Kelly's memory and
apprehend the real killer.

cast
Adrian Dunbar
Kelly
Kika Markham
Anne Appleby
John Grillo
Simon Appleby
Ian Mercer
DS Giggs
Nicholas Woodeson
Hennessy
Don Henderson
Hennessy Sr
David Crellin
Quinlan
Louise Downie
Jacqui Appleby
Ron Meadows
Roberts
Kerry Shale
scene of crime expert
Kathy Jamieson
Jo
Peter Faulkner
Mike
Paul Copley
pathologist
Carol Kidd
nightclub singer
Paulette Constable
waitress
Jeffrey Robert
head of psychology
Julie Westwood
PR woman
Vanessa Kirkpatrick
newscaster
Renny Krupinski
voice expert
Philippa Howell
Dr Turner
Alan David
Hanrahan
Tony Xu
Dr Soraya
Sunatra Sarker
receptionist

Seamus O'Neill
DC Jones
Fine-Time Fontayne
bookie
Danny Davies
ticket inspector
Andy Devine
guard on train
Vincent Paul Davies
taxi driver
Andrew Brittain
presenter
Amanda Loy-Ellis
girl on train
Alan Partington
Mr Hobbs
Romy Baskerville
Irene Hobbs
Daryl Fishwick
Mrs Forbes
Rob Palmer
horse racing commentator
Nelson Fletcher
custody sergeant

2 to say i love you
Middle-class rebel Tina meets
shy stammerer Sean, and the
two begin a passionate affair,
which turns violent when Sean
kills a loan shark. Fitz realises
that two killers were involved,
but the police are unconvinced
until Sean and Tina claim their
second victim, DS Giggs. Tina
attempts to seduce Fitz in a bar,
but he summons the police.
Sean flees to Tina's parents'
home, taking her blind sister,
Sammy, hostage. Fitz manages
to free Sammy, but cannot
prevent Sean from killing
himself in a gas explosion.

cast
Ian Mercer
DS Giggs
Susan Lynch
Tina Brien
Andrew Tiernan
Sean Kerrigan
Susan Vidler
Sammy
David Haig
Graham

144

Beryl Reid
Fitz's mum
Timothy Barlow
Judith's father
Patti Love
Mrs Brien
Keith Ladd
Mr Brien
Gavin Muir
Cormack
Eve Bland
Mrs Cormack
Daniel Green
waiter
Stan Finni
Sergeant Smith
Sarah Keyzor
Nikki Price
Terry Gilligan
Lenny Lion
Reg Stewart
neighbour
Ruth Holden
lady on bus
Margo Stanley
lady on bus
Olivia Jardith
magistrate
Kate Hunt
Mrs Rivers
Glenn Cunningham
Mr Rivers
Rose English
pathologist
Richard Stone
shop manager
James Quinn
doorman
Daniel Green
waiter
Al T. Kossy
expert in pub
Owen Brenman
businessman/Haig
Parvez Quadir
petrol station assistant
Giles Aldershaw
man in house
Tasmin Heatley
woman in house
Jonathan Wrather
Sammy's boyfriend
Steve Halliwell
fire officer

3 one day a lemming will fly
Young Timothy Lang is found hanging in woodland. Suspicion falls on his English teacher, Nigel Cassidy, particularly after he makes two unsuccessful suicide attempts. Meanwhile, public feeling is running high, and Bilborough badly mismanages a near-riot outside the police station. Following an attack on his home, Cassidy is installed in a hotel, where Fitz eventually convinces him to confess. Later, however, Cassidy reveals that his confession was untrue. Horrified, Fitz tries to persuade Bilborough to reopen the investigation, but the DCI refuses to back down.

cast
Christopher Fulford
Nigel Cassidy
Frances Tomelty
Julie Lang
Tim Healy
Mr Lang
Lee Philip Hartney
Andy Lang
John Vine
Lindsay
Wesley Cook
Tim Lang
Linda Henry
Mrs Perry
John Graham Davies
Francis Bates
Amelia Bullmore
Catriona Bilborough
Trevyn McDowell
Leslie
Stan Finni
Sergeant Smith
Ann Francis
croupier
Geoffrey Hutchings
pathologist
Tom Irwin
bully boy

series two
regular cast
Robbie Coltrane
Fitz
Geraldine Somerville
DS Penhaligon
Barbara Flynn
Judith Fitzgerald
Lorcan Cranitch
DS Beck
Ricky Tomlinson
DCI Wise
Kieran O'Brien
Mark Fitzgerald
Tess Thomson
Katie Fitzgerald
Colin Tierney
DC Harriman
Wilbert Johnson
PC Skelton
Isobel Middleton
Catriona Bilborough [4, 6]

4 to be a somebody
Overcome with grief after his father's death, Albie Kinsella kills a Pakistani newsagent then embarks on a murder spree to avenge the dead of the Hillsborough stadium disaster. A serious error by Beck leaves Albie free, and he manages to kill Bilborough before being apprehended. Interrogated by Fitz, Albie eventually reveals the location of his buried fourth victim, but the bomb he has planted there fails to inflict casualties. Fitz discovers a letter bomb addressed to DS Beck just in time, but former *Sun* journalist Clare Moody is not so lucky.

cast
Robert Carlyle
Albie
Beth Goddard
Clare Moody
Tracy Gillman
Jill Kinsella
Gemma Phoenix
Ruth Kinsella
Badi Uzzaman
Shahid Ali

145

Paul Copley
pathologist
Edward Peel
Chief Superintendent
Dave Bond
factory supervisor
Martin Pearson
factory worker
Shango Baku
Gregson
Kim Vithana
Razia Ali
Elaine Heywood
Mrs Ali
Glyn Grain
Professor Nolan
Tricia Hitchcock
Mrs Nolan
Tony Barton
builder
Mike Kelly
Peter Lloyd
John Capps
1st skinhead
Ken Christiansen
2nd skinhead
Marc Seymour
3rd skinhead
Rebecca Clay
counter clerk
John Pickles
neighbour
Peter Clifford
doctor
Rosa Roberts
householder
Jon Huyton
barman
Tony Peers
man in Albie's street
Frankie Jordan
first woman
Sandra Gough
second woman
June Broughton
woman shopper
Ryan Cooper
Baby Bilborough
Philip Childs
radio operator
John Henshaw
quarry foreman
David Holt
hospital administrator

Johnny Leeze
1st Manchester Utd fan
Luke Scott Edwards
2nd Manchester Utd fan
Kevin Quarmby
1st steward

5 the big crunch
The leaders of the cultish
Fellowship of Souls – Kenneth
Trant, wife Virginia, brother
Michael and Michael's wife
Norma – kidnap pregnant
seventeen-year-old schoolgirl
Joanne when she threatens to
reveal her affair with Kenneth.
They drug and attempt to
dispose of her, but she is
released by Michael's autistic
young assistant, Dean. Joanne
dies in hospital, and a confused
Dean confesses to her murder
before hanging himself. DCI
Wise wants the case closed, but
Fitz and Penhaligon, now
beginning an affair, buy time
and eventually expose Kenneth
at a Fellowship meeting, with
Michael's help.

cast
Jim Carter
Kenneth Trant
Maureen O'Brien
Virginia Trant
Cherith Mellor
Norma Trant
James Fleet
Michael Trant
Samantha Morton
Joanne Barnes
Darren Tighe
Dean Saunders
Ellie Haddington
Mrs Barnes
Roger Sloman
Mr Barnes
Nicholas Blane
Father O'Ryan
Emma Cunniffe
Sarah Jennings
Samia Ghadie
Rosie
Doc O'Brien
bus driver

Rosemary Chamney
school secretary
Andy Abrahams
police officer
Lottie Ward
nurse
Nick Fry
doctor
Jeffrey Longmore
local PC

6 men should weep
Floyd, a young mixed-race
cab-driver with a resentment of
white men, rapes his boss's
wife, one of a series of masked
attacks. He is arrested but
dismissed as a suspect. Later,
Penhaligon is raped,
apparently by the same man.
Fitz, however, thinks otherwise,
certain that the serial rapist is
black, unlike her attacker.
Inadvertently encouraged by
Fitz, Floyd kills his next victim.
Penhaligon identifies her rapist
as Beck. As she undertakes her
own investigation, Floyd
targets Judith, but is overcome
by Fitz and Mark. Penhaligon,
meanwhile, holds Beck at
gunpoint.

cast
Graham Aggrey
Floyd Malcolm
Marian McLoughlin
Catherine Carter
John McArdle
Tom Carter
Rachel Davies
Mrs Malcolm
Julie Saunders
Bev Malcolm
Alexander Newland
Marvin Malcolm
Ludmilla Vuli
Trish
Marianne Jean-Baptiste
Marcia Reid
Andrew Readman
Andrew Wiley
Claire Hackett
Deborah Wiley

Gerard O'Hare
O'Rourke
Tony Rohr
Molloy
Diane O'Kelly
Helen Robins
John Middleton
Jed Robins
Ewen Cummins
Wilson Parry
Angela Wynter
Barbara Charles
Jack Randle
taxi driver
Darren Brown
priest
Ina Clough
elderly dancer
Clare Beck
doctor
Stefan Escreet
doctor
Joe Simpson
taxi inspector
Anna Welsh
nosey neighbour
Fiona Allen
house owner

series three
regular cast
Robbie Coltrane
Fitz
Geraldine Somerville
DS Penhaligon
Barbara Flynn
Judith Fitzgerald
Ricky Tomlinson
DCI Wise
Robert Cavanah
DC Temple
Clive Russell
Danny
Kieran O'Brien
Mark Fitzgerald
Tess Thomson
Katie Fitzgerald
Wilbert Johnson
PC Skelton

7 brotherly love
David Harvey murders a
prostitute when he is unable to
pay her. While he is in custody
another prostitute is killed; Fitz

suspects his brother, Father
Michael. Under Fitz's
aggressive interrogation, Beck
admits raping Penhaligon, but
swears Fitz to secrecy.
Meanwhile, Fitz buries his
mother and greets a new son. A
third prostitute is killed, and
David's wife, Maggie, is caught
attacking another. She
confesses to all three murders,
forcing the police to release
David. Incensed, Beck kidnaps
David and pushes him to his
death from a high rooftop,
before jumping himself in front
of a distraught Penhaligon.

cast
Mark Lambert
David Harvey
Bríd Brennan
Maggie Harvey
David Calder
Michael Harvey
Polly Hemingway
Denise Fletcher
Ruth Sheen
Jean McIlvanney
Paul Copley
pathologist
Ron Donachie
Barney
Isobel Middleton
Catriona Bilborough
Sharon Percy
Joyce Watkins
Irene Marot
Paula
Claire Stephanie Hardacre
Joan Harvey
Leanne Molloy
Theresa Harvey
Andrew Whyment
Matthew Harvey
Andrew Knott
Joe Harvey
Dan Armour
man at cashpoint
Barbara Young
Helen McIlvanney
Owen Aaronovitch
Charnock
Gemma Peacock Wood
Jean's daughter

Edward Peel
Chief Superintendent
Stephen Tomlin
DNA expert
Rodney Litchfield
taxi driver
Michael Atkinson
officer
Fergus Colville
man on tram
Meriel Schofield
midwife

8 best boys
Seventeen-year-old care-home
runaway Bill Nash hooks up
with factory foreman Grady.
When Grady's landlady
assumes it's a gay affair, and
the two kill her and go on the
run. Bill runs into his one-time
foster mother, Diane, and
confronts her and her family;
social worker McVerry
intervenes and is murdered.
Bill is later injured, and Grady
captured. Now desperate, Bill
kidnaps Diane and her son at a
fairground. Fitz persuades
Grady to express his love for
the boy, but Bill is killed by
police snipers before he can
surrender.

cast
Liam Cunningham
Grady
John Simm
Bill
Aisling O'Sullivan
Aileen
Annette Ekblom
Diane Nash
John Langford
Brian Nash
Jackie Downey
Mrs Franklin
David Hill
Mr Franklin
Paul Barber
Ian McVerry
Will Knightley
pathologist
Edward Peel
Chief Supt

147

Carla Richee
Gloria
Anthony Lewis
Steven Nash
Dominic Rigby
Philip Nash
Susie Yannis
Linda
Steve Money
cutter
Jane Wheldon
Janet Emery
Jim Whelan
foreman
Katherine Dow Blyton
doctor

9 true romance
University technician Janice
develops an obsessive love for
Fitz, seducing and murdering a
series of male students to
attract his attention.
Persuaded by Penhaligon, Fitz
agrees to be 'fired' from the
investigation to bring her into
the open. Janice kidnaps Mark,
then gives herself up, refusing
to reveal his whereabouts. Fitz
discovers that she is consumed
with bitterness at the
knowledge that her father
abused her two sisters but not
her. Mark is rescued just in
time, but though Fitz shares
Judith's relief, he refuses to
commit himself to her.

cast
Emily Joyce
Janice
Rosemary Martin
Irene Jackson
Katie Purslow
Louise
Kenneth Gilbert
father
Fleur Bennett
Nena
Kevin Dignam
Colin
Liz Estensen
Reenie Wise
Larry Waller
Dave

Ian Curtis
John Branaghan
Biddy Hodson
Carol Barker
Alan Maher
Frank Weetman
Iain Mitchell
vice-chancellor
Jan Linnik
student
Will Knightley
pathologist
Jane Lowe
landlady
Peter Lorenzelli
dog owner
Alan Maher
Frank Weetman
Hetta Charnley
Maureen Kiernan
Kay Purcell
TV reporter voice-over

White Ghost
United Kingdom/1996

directed by
Richard Standeven
executive producers
Gub Neal
For A & E Network:
Delia Fine
producer
Hilary Bevan Jones
written by
Paul Abbott
director of photography
Dick Dodd
film editor
Tony Cranstoun
production designer
Chris Wilkinson
music composed by
Rick Wentworth

© Granada Television
production company
Granada Television
in association with A & E
Network

production executive
Craig McNeil
production supervisor
Bill Leather

Hong Kong:
Neil Macdonald
production co-ordinator
Karen Barker
Hong Kong:
Melissa Dice
production manager
John Rushton
location manager
Ben Rimmer
Hong Kong:
Yau Ming Joseph
production secretary
Jo Farr
assistant directors
1st: Peter Shaw
2nd: Claire McCourt
continuity
Joyce Kitchen
casting
Marilyn Johnson
Andrew Hall
additional casting (Hong Kong)
Pat Pao
April Webster
script associate
Catriona McKenzie
camera operator
Mike Miller
focus puller
Richard Brierley
grips
Mike Fisher
Gary Stanton
Hong Kong:
Deki Lee Chuwing
steadicam operator
Alf Tramontin
assistant film editors
David Boyle
Chris Clarkson
art directors
Dave Butterworth
Hong Kong:
Chiu Kin Sun
graphic designer
Philip Buckley
production buyer
David Livsey
Hong Kong:
Chan Yee
costume designer
Tudor George
wardrobe supervisor
Michael Richards

make-up design
Sue Milton
Anastasia Shirley
sound mixer
Nick Steer
dubbing mixer
John Whitworth
dubbing editor
John Senior
Mark Briscoe
stunt co-ordinator (Hong Kong)
Mark King

Essex-born Dennis Philby kills a Hong Kong business rival; Fitz, on a lecture tour, is enlisted by local police. Fitz asks for Penhaligon, but gets Wise instead. Dennis discovers that pregnant girlfriend Su Lin is planning a termination and kills the abortionist, then imprisons her in a shipping container, where he marries her in a bogus ceremony. Dennis is captured and Su Lin presumed dead, but Fitz believes otherwise, and the police arrange to 'release' Dennis, then follow him to the dockyards. Fitz rescues Su Lin, but cannot prevent Dennis's suicide.

cast
Robbie Coltrane
Fitz
Ricky Tomlinson
DCI Wise
Freda Foh Shen
DCI Janet Lee Cheung
Barnaby Kay
Dennis Philby
Michael Pennington
Commander Gordon Ellison
Liu Jo Ying
Su Lin
David Tse
junior detective
Tom Wu
detective lawyer
Zoe Hart
Catherine Wilson
Dennis Chan
Freddie

Mark Hadfield
Gerald Freeman
Glen Goei
Dr Sunny
Pik-Sen Lim
Wei Wei
David Bradley
Frank Carter
Benedict Wong
Peter Yang
Stuart Ong
pathologist
Chaplin Chang
hotel manager
Choy-Ling Man
nurse
Claudia Malkovich
secretary
Cecil Chang
Al Tang
Ng Wah Sun
bellboy
Aleck Woo
young copper
Chan Chi Fai Sunny
observer on helicopter
Elvis Mok Kwok Kwang
marksman on helicopter

Cracker
United Kingdom/2006

director
Antonia Bird
executive producer
Andy Harries
producer
John Chapman
written by
Jimmy McGovern
director of photography
Florian Hoffmeister
production designer
Tom Bowyer
film editor
Chris Barwell
composers
Stephen Morris
Gillian Gilbert

© Granada Television
production company
ITV Productions

line producer
Louise Mutter

production co-ordinators
Monique Mussell
Zoë Edwards
post-production supervisor
Jane Coombes
head of production
Marigo Kehoe
production executive
Gary Connelly
unit manager
Sally Maynard
location manager
Bridget Kenningham
production secretary
Sarah Lindfield
production accountants
Adrian O'Brien
assistant directors
1st: Radford Neville
2nd: Tom Rye
script supervisor
Jane Burrows
script executive
Roxy Spencer
dialogue editor
Richard Dunford
casting director
Andy Pryor
focus puller
Craig Feather
grip
Richard Griffiths
stills photography
Neil Marland
Brian Moody
Rachel Joseph
Paul Jones
assistant film editor
Danielle Palmer
art director
Anna Pritchard
production buyer
Ussal Smithers
prop master
Paul Carter
effects editor
Peter Baldock
online editor/VFX editor
Scott Hinchcliffe
VFX editor
Shane Warden
titles and graphics
Central Station Technicolour
costume designer
Rhona Russell

149

costume supervisor
Sally Campbell
make-up designer
Jessica Taylor
hair and make-up artist
Juliet Jackson
make-up artist
Angela Parkinson
additional music
Corker Conboy
sound recordist
Dennis Cartwright
sound maintenance
John Coates
Chris Cartwright
dubbing mixer
Tim Alban
stunt co-ordinator
Gary Connery

Fitz returns to Manchester from Australia for Katy's wedding in time to join the investigation into an American comedian's murderer. The killer is Kenny, an ex-soldier turned policeman tortured by memories of Northern Ireland, who later kills the comedian's wealthy stepfather and a drug addict who was attempting to blackmail him. Fitz suspects Kenny, but cannot make him confess. At breaking point, Kenny holes up at his home with a gun and his own children as hostages. Fitz attempts to negotiate, but Kenny is ultimately shot by a police sniper.

Robbie Coltrane
Edward Fitzgerald
Barbara Flynn
Judith Fitzgerald
Kieran O'Brien
Mark Fitzgerald
Anthony Flanagan
Kenny Archer
Richard Coyle
DI Walters
Nisha Nayar
DS Saffron Saleh
Rafe Spall
DS McAllister

Leo Gregory
wallet thief
Lisa Eichhorn
Jean Molloy
Sara Roache
chief super
Stefanie Willmore
Katie Fitzgerald
John Evans
James Fitzgerald
Andrea Lowe
Elaine
Matt Rippy
American comedian
Demetri Goritsas
Harry Peters
Katy Cavanagh
Helen
Danny Cunningham
Bob
Angelo Dommino
Gregory, the groom
Stephen MacKenna
Robert, groom's father
Rosina Carbone
Maria Fitzgerald
Christine Barton
Elaine's mother
Lilla-Ella Kelleher
Mark's daughter
Joel Davies
Daniel Archer
Charlotte Forsyth
Amy Archer
Nathan Tunner
Jake Archer
Michael Boddimeade
young man
Adam Zane
comedy club manager
Andrew Norris
Mr Thorpe
Mark Hallett
police officer
Hester Ullyart
Rachel
David Parker
nosey neighbour
Ralph Casson
taxi driver 1
Moey Hassan
taxi driver 2
Steven Farebrother
Fitz's taxi driver

transmission history
series one
the mad woman in the attic
episode 1 ITV
27 September 1993
(22.00–23.00)
episode 2 ITV
4 October 1993
(22.00–23.00)

to say i love you
episode 1 ITV
11 October 1993
(22.00–23.00)
episode 2 ITV
18 October 1993
(22.00–23.00)
episode 2 ITV
25 October 1993
(22.00–23.00)

one day a lemming will fly
episode 1 ITV
1 November 1993
(22.00–23.00)
episode 2 ITV
8 November 1993
(22.00–23.00)

series two
to be a somebody
episode 1 ITV
10 October 1994
(22.00–23.00)
episode 2 ITV
17 October 1994
(22.00–23.00)
episode 3 ITV
24 October 1994
(22.00–23.00)

the big crunch
episode 1 ITV
31 October 1994
(22.00–23.00)
episode 2 ITV
7 November 1994
(22.00–23.00)
episode 3 ITV
14 November 1994
(22.00–23.00)

150

men should weep
episode 1 ITV
21 November 1994
(22.00–23.00)
episode 2 ITV
28 November 1994
(22.00–23.00)
episode 3 ITV
5 December 1994
(22.00–23.00)

series three
brotherly love
episode 1 ITV
22 October 1995
(21.00–22.15)
episode 2 ITV
23 October 1995
(22.00–23.00)

episode 3 ITV
30 October 1995
(22.00–23.00)

best boys
episode 1 ITV
6 November 1995
(22.00–23.00)
episode 2 ITV
13 November 1995
(22.00–23.00)

true romance
episode 1 ITV
20 November 1995
(22.00–23.00)
episode 2 ITV
27 November 1995
(22.00–23.00)

specials
white ghost ITV
28 October 1996
cracker ITV1
1 October 2006

Index

153

154

Also Published:

Buffy the Vampire Slayer
Anne Billson

Civilisation
Jonathan Conlin

CSI: Crime Scene Investigation
Steven Cohan

Doctor Who
Kim Newman

Edge of Darkness
John Caughie

The League of Gentlemen
Leon Hunt

The Likely Lads
Phil Wickham

The Office
Ben Walters

Our Friends in the North
Michael Eaton

Queer as Folk
Glyn Davis

Seinfeld
Nicholas Mirzoeff

Seven Up
Stella Bruzzi

The Singing Detective
Glen Creeber

Star Trek
Ina Rae Hark